Not f*cking ready to adult.

A totally ill-informed guide to life

Iain Stirling

HarperCollins*Publishers*

HarperCollins*Publishers*
1 London Bridge Street
London SE1 9GF

www.harpercollins.co.uk

First published by HarperCollins*Publishers* 2018 as
Not Ready to Adult Yet
This edition published 2019

1 3 5 7 9 10 8 6 4 2

A catalogue record of this book is
available from the British Library

ISBN 978-0-00-828801-3

Printed and bound in Great Britain by
CPI Group (UK) Ltd, Croydon, CR0 4YY

To my mum Alison, my dad Rodger and my sister Kirsten. This book isn't for you, it's because of you. I love you.

CONTENTS

adulting

NOUN
informal

The practice of behaving in a way characteristic of a responsible adult, especially the accomplishment of mundane but necessary tasks.

However, the entire time you are carrying out said tasks you are uncomfortably aware that you have no idea what the hell you are doing, you will fuck it up and eventually be found out.

*'**Fucking hell**, this adulting is* **IMPOSSIBLE**. *How do I explain to my boss that I'm late for work because I dropped my phone in the toilet while watching a YouTube video and taking a shit?'*

WHAT IT MEANS TO
BE AN ADULT

I'm constantly told by my parents, friends and my birth certificate that I'm an adult now, but what does that even mean? And why does it seem to be so insanely difficult? Following some in-depth research/googling I have ascertained that, generally speaking, the idea of being an adult is split into two camps, that of the 'responsible adult' and the 'irresponsible adult'. These two definitions are as follows.

Responsible adult: taking on the new-found responsibilities that come with being a grown-up, such as getting a job, buying a house and having children.

Irresponsible adult: now the restrictions of childhood have been removed you can do or act however you want. For example, staying up as late as you like, drinking alcohol, spending your money as you choose.

Whether 'responsible' or 'irresponsible', these actions carry with them that bizarre feeling of, 'Wow, I'm being such an adult right now.' I've listed a few of my favourite such moments that make you feel like a grown-up here:

- COOKING MEALS FROM SCRATCH
- GOING ON HOLIDAY *WITHOUT* YOUR PARENTS
- DRIVING, PARTICULARLY DURING A TRICKY PARALLEL PARK
- FIRST TIME YOU GO INTO YOUR OVERDRAFT (LOSES ITS ALLURE QUICKLY)
- REALISING YOU CAN EAT OUT EVEN IF IT ISN'T A SPECIAL OCCASION
- BEING IN THE SUPERMARKET AND REALISING YOU CAN BUY WHATEVER YOU LIKE
- DEFROSTING A FREEZER
- DRIVING THROUGH A CITY CENTRE AND BEING ABLE TO CONFIDENTLY STATE, 'THAT USED TO BE A BLOCKBUSTERS'
- LIKING COLDPLAY
- BEING ABLE TO LEGALLY RENT A VAN
- BEING TOLD TO TURN THE VOLUME DOWN BY YOUR NEIGHBOURS RATHER THAN YOUR PARENTS
- IRONING YOUR FIRST SHIRT
- HAVING A NIGHT OUT THAT DOESN'T INVOLVE PRE-DRINKING
- THE FIRST TIME YOU REALISE YOU LIKE OLIVES

- HAVING A COFFEE INSTEAD OF A DESSERT
- HELPING YOUR PARENTS PICK UP SOMETHING THAT'S HEAVY
- WHEN YOU'RE HUNGRY AND WAITING FOR SOMEONE TO COOK YOU DINNER THEN REALISE THAT SOMEONE IS YOU
- MAKING PEOPLE TAKE THEIR SHOES OFF BEFORE COMING INTO YOUR HOUSE
- WHEN BANK HOLIDAYS BECOME A CHANCE TO CARRY OUT CHORES, NOT NURSE HANGOVERS

I ONCE TOLD AN EIGHT-YEAR-OLD TO GO FUCK HIMSELF

A few years ago now I told an eight-year-old to go fuck himself. That moment was unintentional and clearly unfortunate, but it would go on to help me haul myself from a malaise I had found myself in for a number of years. Like many of life's significant events, I was worryingly unaware of its importance, as is the case with the majority of life-changing moments: applying for a job, meeting the person who goes on to be your significant other or even buying that leather jacket that remains, to this day, a real staple in your wardrobe. It was just another moment like all the others; in fact, minutes before, I was sitting backstage at yet another gig, readying myself to perform to a new group of strangers like I do every night of the week.

What was it then about that particular night that sticks so solidly in my psyche like an annoying bit of apple skin between teeth? The fact I swore in a child's face certainly adds to the level of permanence afforded to that particular memory, but it's not just the extreme embarrassment of the situation. Only last year I walked into a hotel room where a businessman was taking a shit, where I told him my full name and then left. Although that incident still haunts me today – and I'm assuming that businessman – it is this particular gig that always comes to me in my moments of solitude. In the shower, just before I go to bed, when I'm on a train with only a podcast and my own thoughts to keep me company. Boom! There it is. That little voice hidden in the depths of my mind pops in to quickly remind me of that evening.

'Hello, Iain. Remember that time you told an eight-year-old to go fuck himself? You do? Oh good. Well, have a nice night.'

I certainly could have been in a better place, being recently single, technically speaking 'out of work' (though financially buoyant) and, most crucially, unfulfilled. That's the big one. You ever felt like that? Even though on the face of it life is good – your work is tolerable, bordering on enjoyable, your social life is filled with interesting and entertaining friends, and your family are as supportive and loving as ever – for some reason there is that niggling feeling deep down in the depths of your soul that something's not quite right, something's missing. You feel like a selfish prick for even entertaining it; you have everything you've ever needed and so many people have made so many sacrifices so that you could have it, but 'it' isn't enough and you can't for the life of you work out why.

What the fuck even is 'it' and why can't I just have 'it'? 'It' is like *The X Factor* of life satisfaction, but none of us seem to have the Simon Cowell-esque ability to identify it correctly; it always seems to narrowly pass us by. There is nothing you can do to help identify it more clearly – literally nothing. I even spent a month with my shirt unbuttoned offensively low and my trousers pulled embarrassingly high. It didn't help – I just got funny looks.

For years I was told by friends, family, school teachers, colleges and even social media that I was special and destined for great things. I'm fully aware that's not unique to me, by the way. I'm sure you too have been awarded certificates at school and told how beautiful you are in Facebook comments, as we live in a world where praise is constantly heaped onto everyone. Despite this wall of positive encouragement, however, in the specific moment I swore at an eight-year-old, I just felt like another cog in the machine, another Starbucks-drinking, McDonald's-munching face in the crowd.

To some of you this lack of fulfilment will resonate; to others, however, it will sound ungrateful, an odd note on which to start a book. I'm fully aware that many of you will be reading this on your holidays: you've found a sun lounger, bought your fruity cocktail, taken the obligatory photo of your legs with the ocean as their beautiful backdrop and posted it online with the sole intention of mocking your friends who are currently dragging their sorry asses into the office for another torturous Monday. You've then opened this book and thought, 'Fuck me, this *Love Island* prick's a bit down in the dumps.' Fear ye not, my ITV2-loving amigos, for this book is about optimism and 'living your best life', as is famously said by tedious people on Twitter – and now me, apparently. Not to mention the story of me telling that eight-year-old to go fuck himself is in fact a bloody doozy – so there is plenty to look forward to!

WHAT THE HELL IS THIS?

Despite heavy reliance on my own personal experience – I mean, 'myself' is what I know best, the only thing I can truly call myself 'an expert' in – this book will not be an autobiographical romp through my life to date. I've not done enough stuff yet. You gotta think word count. I would really have to drag out that time I went caravanning with Pam and Bill in order to achieve anything other than pamphlet status. And no one wants to hear about that holiday. A boy called Craig chopped a wasp in half but otherwise it was largely uneventful.

Instead I'll talk about my generation – millennials. They've got loads of stories. They'll know loads of Craigs. Craigs who'll have done things other than demonstrate serial-killer tendencies during a long weekend in Moffat. The millennial was born between roughly 1981 and 2002, basically (although not exclusively) old enough to remember what they were up to during 9/11 but too old to grasp the notion of watching young lads with mad fringes playing the computer game *Minecraft* on YouTube. It's a generation famed – should the copious Buzz-Feed articles be believed – for failing to grow up, never being able to properly 'adult'.

That's me, I'm like that, but why are we *all* perceived this way? If that's also you then strap in. If it's not then don't you worry your non-millennial head. Most of the stuff I'm going to talk about here is universal and hopefully funny regardless of the digits you have etched onto your birth certificate. As well as talking about my generation, I will also talk *to* my generation, in a series of conversations with fellow millennials about their own personal journey through life, their hopes and fears, and the lessons they have learnt on their path to adulthood. A few of them have got well over a million followers on Instagram, so that will be bloody exciting.

I hope that through the process of researching and writing about my generation I will better understand how we work, and as a result better understand myself. Why was that night I swore at a child such a pivotal point in my personal development? Why does that precious 'it' always manage to slip me by no matter how much luck is thrown my way? And, believe me, luck is what we all have in abundance, even if it doesn't always feel like it. You are lucky. You're reading this book, which means you're most likely from a first-world country, one of those that allows freedom of speech and has sufficient educational facilities to make literacy the norm, and you even have enough expendable income to be able to buy this in the first place – unless you've nicked it, of course. We're bloody lucky and privileged and all the rest, yet sometimes it doesn't feel enough. Why? What are we so scared of?

FAILURE IS NOT AN OPTION

That night stays with me to this day for the simple reason that it was the first time in my short lifespan that one of my biggest fears became a reality – a fear all millennials share when it comes to life: the fear of doing it wrong. Fucking up. Becoming an adult is scary and easy to get wrong, so this fear of fucking it up hangs over us like a rain cloud hangs over a cartoon character having a bad day. University costs a fortune, reality-TV stars are millionaires by the age of 21 and everyone on social media seems to be smashing life (as well as avocados). So if you take a wrong turn at any point, well, why did you even bother? Success has changed from a marathon to a sprint and the starting line is very much over-capacity. You'd better make it to the finish and you'd better do it quick! I mean, who wants success in their fifties? You can't even look good in the photos.

The really weird thing is that for years failure was seen as a necessary rite of passage to success. Like many of you reading this I can often find myself deep in a late-night YouTube hole. And when I'm properly stuck down there, one of my most common places of solace, after blackheads being popped and kittens performing on musical instruments, is the inspirational talk, normally a celebrity collecting an honorary degree with a rolled-up certificate in one hand, a funny hat on his or her head and some inspirational music in the background, which I do hope was added in after. I mean, surely even the most wet-behind-the-ears graduate would realise the ridiculous levels of self-importance attached to bringing your own Enya CD to a university speech. Anyway, the point is that during these talks failure is hyped up beyond belief, fetishised to the young people in the slightly less funny hats who look up in awe.

These stories begin in various ways: 'I didn't land my first proper acting job until I was 40,' 'I had several failed companies before making my millions aged 55,' 'I sawed my own arm off with a penknife.' Yet despite the severity and diversity of the challenges our speakers have faced, they always end the same ... 'But look at me now.' You don't get much more adult than that! Standing in front of an audience being open and frank about all your failings but still managing to have achieved something special – now *that* is good-quality adulting.

Failure today, however, simply isn't an option. You must succeed young, without any periods spent on the dole and ideally with all your limbs still attached. Failure to meet this new-found desire to succeed quickly leaves us in a constant state of flux, doubting our every decision. It still blows my mind when I'm watching some reality TV show and I see a 14-year-old being interviewed backstage saying something like 'I've been working my whole life for this' or 'This is my one shot.' I feel like grabbing them and screaming, 'There's no rush – when I was 14 I was sitting in a caravan watching someone chop a wasp in half!'

Despite the knowledge that time is on my side I have those moments of doubt every day; sometimes it's a light murmur under the surface and other times it's debilitating in its severity, but it's always there. The feeling that I'm not good enough, I've not achieved enough, I'm not happy enough, that's not good enough, they're not good enough, I'm not thin enough, my photos don't get liked enough, my job isn't impressive enough, I don't earn enough and so on. It will continue, I imagine, until death. Sweet, blissful death. And even then I'll be thinking, 'Oh Christ, I've only gone and died – this is embarrassing.'

As depressing as it may sound, these worries are necessary for our journey into adulthood. Without a fear of failure or a desire to achieve we would all just coast along, never really achieving anything. We've all got that mate who's seemingly happy all the time. Who wants to be like them? They're creepy – constantly smiling, never hungover, big fan of their boss, constantly eating 'superfoods'. Get in the bin. I'd rather be in a Wetherspoons chatting to my equally hungover friend Karen about how Jim from accounts is a fucking prick, his eyes are too close together, I hate those 'wacky ties he wears' and 'correctomundo' isn't an actual word, it's a waste of oxygen.

Young people today seem to fail to realise how young they actually are. If you are under the age of 25 you have no fucking clue how many bites at the cherry you actually might have. Fuck up a bit. It's really important. Fuck up. Hell, if you're reading this on a bus, punch the person sitting next to you. You could go to jail for two years, get out and still be eligible for a young person's railcard. You are so young. Yet despite this knowledge of our youth, a fear of failing is what seems to pin our generation down. Anyway, enough waffle, let's get started.

Here we go – an adult man who once feared failure, avoided it at all costs, will now retell each and every failure he's ever had to you, the reader, so you can realise that maybe failure isn't all that bad.

CHAPTER 1

BAD PARENTING

Mollycoddled

When you watch as much *Love Island* as I'm contractually required to do, you really do start to become enthralled by every single minute of it. Don't get me wrong, there are downsides. I mean, essentially I am paid to sit in a small booth while a bunch of young people go into a villa and, well, fuck each other, and then I ... watch. For ages. For too long, you might even say. That's how I pay my mortgage. Worse still, my parents have seen to it that my overly supportive millennial upbringing didn't end at the point I left home for London to become a stand-up – not a chance. My parents still keep every cutting, record every show and retweet every bit of praise I receive on their own custom-made Twitter accounts, or 'Iain Shrines' as they hate that I call them. My dad's account is the very cleverly named MySonDoesJokes – give him a follow, he'd bloody love that. My sister is a bit angry about it, but

MyDaughterDoesMediaManagement doesn't quite have the same ring.

Having supportive parents is wonderful but somewhat annoying for me as an artist. I mean, all good art comes from pain – great artists have suffered and then told their stories to the world through their chosen medium. Thanks to Alison and Rodger being bloody saints means I've had none of that. I'm trying to write a book here, Mum and Dad, can you please give me something to work with? They haven't even had a divorce, the selfish pricks! I've tried everything to get something out of them but they are simply too good.

'Fuck you, Mum and Dad, I'm going to go be a comedian.'

'Great! We can drive you to all your gigs.'

'You are missing the point!'

The issue with my supportive parents – other than a lack of exposure to failure, the creation in my head of an imaginary safety net and an inflated sense of self-worth, all of which we will get round to talking about very soon – is the fact that when I say my parents watch everything, I do mean *everything*. Being the voice of *Love Island* and knowing that your parents watch is like being a kid watching a film with your parents when a raunchy sex scene would come on (my most vivid memory was the scene in *Braveheart*; at one point you see actual boobage – as a pre-teen I was in bits!) and you had that horrible moment of knowing that you and your parents were watching sex together, they knew they were watching sex with their child and the whole family would just sit in silence as Mel Gibson had his merry way with Catherine

McCormack. Everyone would be transfixed by the screen, which by this time was absolutely covered in people having sex – it looked like the inside of an old phone box coated in those sex-line phone cards. The ones where you phone up and someone talks dirty down the phone to you – or so I've been told.

The entire evening would change from a chilled-out 'movie night' to a social time-bomb waiting to detonate in sexual congress and awkwardness, which would ultimately result in you praying for the sofa to gain sentience and gobble you up whole, or at least take you through to another room where neither your parents nor scenes of any sort of a sexual nature would be present.

Well, thanks to *Love Island* I get that feeling every day for an entire summer. And not only am I watching this with my parents, I'm actually talking them through the entire process. Just me giving my parents a step-by-step breakdown of the filth taking pace before their (and my) very eyes.

'There you go, Father, that's them off to the outside beds ... Now what's happening is that she has gone down there to perform what I believe is called a b –'

Sorry, I can't. I just can't. Anyway, you get the idea – the whole thing can be very grim. The thing I can be grateful for is that when it comes to *Love Island* my parents play a far more passive role in their viewing experience, because normally when it comes to the TV my parents enjoy something much more immersive. One Easter, I had a Saturday night off work, which for a stand-up comedian is very rare.

The upside of my job is that I'm my own boss and have days to myself to do as I please. In the majority of cases this will take the form of sitting in my pants playing *FIFA*, as this pleases me very much. However, the same can't be said for the majority of the population, so as a stand-up comedian you have to work around everyone else's social calendar. This means weekends and bank holidays are not a time to relax and socialise with friends, but instead mean going to theatres to entertain people who want to relax and socialise with theirs. Don't get me wrong, there is a lot of free time being a stand-up comedian, and people often say to me it must be amazing not working during the day – you can just do what you like. And, to be honest, the first few years are incredible. However, after a couple of years or so there are only so many empty pubs you can sit in, or 14-year-old French kids you can smash on *FIFA* before the solitude becomes all too much.

Anyway, the point is I had a very rare Saturday night off, so I decided to spend it training up to Edinburgh to surprise my mum and dad. On arrival I walked into our living room to see my parents watching the television, as is customary on a Saturday night; however, my folks were not sitting on the couch as would be customary. My parents were sitting in the middle of the living room, on office chairs, facing away from the television, just staring at the wall. I approached the two pensioners, my brain quickly trying to work out if I could afford to send them both into homes, and asked them what was going on, to which my mother proudly declared: 'We're watching *The Voice* and playing along at home.'

My parents were watching *The Voice* and only turning around when they liked the voice of the person they were listening to. My mum wasn't best pleased, however, as good old Dad had refused to turn even once, instead spending his Saturday night angrily perched on an old office chair, screaming into a wall: 'Shite, he's shite, she's shite, everyone's shite.' I once mentioned this on Scott Mills's Radio 1 show, and someone texted in to tell me you can also have the same 'play along at home' Saturday night experience by watching *Take Me Out* with friends and giving everyone a torch. I can imagine that really kicking off after a few bottles of wine have been sunk. Give it a go – tweet me the results!

NEVER GO CARAVANNING WITH YOUR PARENTS

Parents often say they want to give their kids everything their own childhood lacked. How many times have you seen some rich rapper in a television interview speaking about how they're going to give their kids 'all the stuff I never had growing up'? But in all honesty does a five-month-old need Gucci slip-ons? Yes, they look cute and durable, but was your childhood irreparably ruined because you didn't have a pair of diamond-encrusted slippers? I actually think it's often the negative experiences of growing up that help shape us. Without the rough do you always appreciate the smooth? I now really appreciate going on proper adult holidays, and that most certainly has a lot to do with my holidays growing up.

You see, as a child my parents made a big decision that would have a massive impact on my life for years to come. A decision more and more couples are making in this modern era. They decided ... to buy a caravan. Yup, every summer Mum, Dad, my sister and me would cram ourselves into a four-berth and head off to Loch Lomond, Aberfeldy, Biggar, Aviemore or some other Scottish holiday destination that sounds less like an exotic getaway than a Middle Earth council estate, where you expect to see a bunch of orcs stealing lead from a roof or a bunch of elves drinking cider in the park, but instead witness old people attending bingo nights and families in tents entertaining themselves with games of charades.

So despite their fantasyland names, they were far from the exciting world of the 'Rohan' Bronx or the 'Gondor' high rises – they were caravan parks. And not just any caravan parks – Scottish caravan parks. The wettest places known to man. If you listen very carefully on arrival to any Scottish caravan park you can actually hear David Attenborough narrating *Blue Planet*. I mean, most kids return from summer holidays with a tan. I would hobble into class with trench foot. Caravans can't deal with the extremity of Scottish weather. This is the sort of weather that requires bricks and mortar. In the story of the three little pigs not one of them chooses to stay in a caravan. Not one. And one of those idiots opted for hay. That means a pig, a fucking pig, looked at a caravan and thought to himself, 'Nah, I'd rather live in a house made of horse food.'

I always think that if you're buying a place of residence, you want to do it somewhere respectable. When we shot off to buy our caravan we went to a field. 'An area of open land, especially one planted with crops or pasture, typically bounded by hedges or fences', that's what the dictionary defines a field as. Not as 'a really brilliant place to buy a respectable house'. I would say the only thing of any value that has been bought in a field is a field.

Once or twice a year the Stirling posse would pack up and head off on our epic adventures to mystical faraway lands, such as Biggar, Forfar, Sandylands – the list goes on, and at no stage improves in quality. The other issue was that we had to drag our place of residence on the back of a clapped-out Ford Escort, meaning that speed was never really our friend. Hours would be spent travelling for very little reward (distance). When you are an excitable child off on their summer holidays, nothing quite takes the gleam off a four-hour car journey more than having your dad trot up a small hill to say to your mum: 'I can see our house from here.' I remember visiting family friends on our 'holidays'. Like casually popping in for the day. On a holiday. It just wasn't right. A holiday destination shouldn't be a place where you can pop in for the day. It's a holiday, not someone's front room. I want to go to Mallorca and join a kids' club run by a depressed actor like all the other normal children!

Now, I don't want to fully destroy the legend that is the family caravan holiday. I've got many happy memories of that place. Yes, it was so cold that I vividly remember my mum having to get more dressed for bed than she had for the hike we had taken earlier that day. Yes, the thing was so small and the beds so close together that every time my dad farted I could genuinely feel my hair blow back. And yes, once I watched a child chop a wasp in half. But there was so much fun to be had fishing, boating, climbing, with the friends we made, the weirdos we met and that time my uncle Bill stopped a family from going home in the middle of the night because they thought a power station was going to blow up. The couple stayed, the power station didn't obliterate us all, everyone was happy!

There is fun to be had in these places, and as a child sometimes it's important to have to go and find it. Similarly, every time I now find myself on a sun lounger in my all-inclusive Spanish holiday resort, I think back to that tiny little Elddis caravan, and with a wry smile on my face take a sip on my Corona and realise how lucky I am. I'm now a great big adult that can decide where I want to go on my holidays, and sorry you have to hear this, Mum and Dad, but it isn't fucking Falkirk.

I'm happy with what I had and delighted with what I've now got. Now that's good parenting. I'm not scarred by the hardships of my childhood holidays, nor am I left with some misplaced sense of entitlement after too many trips to Disneyland as a youngster. And thank God for that, because is there anything on this entire planet more intolerable than a spoilt brat?

I've spent many years working in children's television, and there is nothing more heartbreaking than being told someone important is coming to a filming day and they're bringing their kid with them. I'd like to say at this point that if you're someone high up in the world of kids' TV reading this and you have children and I've met them, this definitely isn't about them. It isn't. This is about those other pricks and their spoilt-rotten little shits. You know the ones I'm talking about? Good, let's talk about them.

When children grow up around children's TV they become the most disruptive little gremlins ever to set foot in a studio. Jaded by the magical world of TV at the age of eight, walking about in a pressed shirt and a pair of chinos like they own the place: 'Mummy, I'm bored, who's he?' I'm a Z-list children's entertainer, you little shit. A lot of this may be me somewhat 'projecting' – as my therapist says, it 100 per cent is – but the point still stands that if you show kids too much of a good thing too young then they may well grow up not appreciating the privileges they have. This could lead to them conducting all sorts of wrongs, for example being rude to one of the greatest BAFTA-award-winning children's TV presenters of all time. I mean, come on, 'Who's he?' Take a running jump, you absolute tool of an eight-year-old. Again, if you work in kids' TV, *definitely* not about your kid. They were lovely.

I don't want this to come across as a weird 'my parents are better than yours' humblebrag, by the way. Similarly, if you missed the irony draped over the whole 'I'm the greatest kids' TV presenter of all time', then that is solely down to my limited writing abilities. I know I'm not the best. I've met Phillip Schofield, Tim Vincent, Dick and Dom, Zoë Ball, Angellica Bell and

Otis the Aardvark – I'm fully aware of the tough competition I'm up against. Let's just say I'm top 10 and move on.

An important factor in becoming an adult is to avoid constantly internalising and comparing other people's lives with your own. As a kid that sort of behaviour used to do you all manner of good: 'But Ahir's parents let him stay up until nine on a Friday.' Boom! Next thing you know you're watching the 'late' film on a Friday night like a proper fucking gangster! Isn't parental guilt a brilliant thing?

Perhaps all our parents did was try to give us the best life possible, and it was us constantly comparing and contrasting with others that created this illusion that we are smothered and over-protected. Parents can't protect their children for ever. I mean, I know eight-year-olds that have been told to go fuck themselves. You need to do your own thing, let others do theirs and hope for the best. I can't beat Otis the Aardvark – he's a talking anteater, for God's sake. I'm merely a talking man. In the hearts of British children I'm always coming off second best in that exchange.

Now that I am an adult, or at least trying my bloody best, I think quite a bit about what was going through my mum's head when she was bringing me up. I'm nearly the same age as she was when she had me. Fuck, I couldn't imagine having a kid right now. Chances are I'd drop it. But she managed it and I've never really asked her how. I had been meaning to interview my mum for ages for this book. I had always managed to find a reason to put it off: it was too late, we were too drunk, my equipment wasn't working properly. I've never actually thought, until right now, why I was so scared to sit my mum down in the podcast chair. I guess it's the intimacy of it that was the real kicker. We'd never talked about anything like that in real detail, and now, like a true millennial, I had decided not only to have the conversation after three decades of my life, but also to record the whole thing. Freud would have had a field day (and not the type where you purchase a caravan). Sure, the microphones are somewhat phallic, but that sick Austrian quack needn't know that.

So despite my reservations and fears about what might be said, I decided to sit down and speak to the main woman herself – Alison Stirling, my mother.

Interview with My Mum –
'I will never make my children old before their time'

ALISON STIRLING

I intended to go back to work, but once I had you I thought, 'No, there is no way. I don't want to do that.' I was kind of brought up in a nursery, and I didn't think we were going to have a family. I was more shocked than anybody that I would want to give up work for it, but that's what I wanted to do and so that's what your dad and I did. That halved the money that came in.

IAIN STIRLING

Yeah, that's why we had to go on caravan
holidays.

ALISON STIRLING

Then Kirsten, your sister, came along 18
months later. The theory was that during the
week I would get everything ready so that
at the weekend we had family time. People
used to say, 'Oh, I can't stand this,' but
I used to say, 'Boring is as boring does.'
And we did a lot. I have to say I felt I
loved it, but –

IAIN STIRLING

And you were brill, this is what I'm saying.

ALISON STIRLING

But at the end of the day there is a danger
that I sometimes think maybe I didn't allow
you to develop, and, you know, there's
always that 'If I'd done this, had I done
that' …

IAIN STIRLING

Develop in terms of, like, independently be
able to do my own stuff?

ALISON STIRLING

Yeah, get up in the morning. That sort of
thing.

IAIN STIRLING

Yeah, this is exactly the point I was going
to make. It's not a bad thing. What I mean
is my childhood was amazing and you're an
amazing mum and Dad's an amazing dad –
parents that you know would lie down in
traffic for you – but then it also means
that when someone says, 'This deadline was
due a week ago,' I'm now the sort of person
to say, 'It will be fine, someone will sort
it out.' Because in my head I'm going,
'Mummy and Daddy will sort it out.' And I
think if I were to have kids I would get
them to do more. But what I'm saying is
that's not bad. The point I'm making is what
was it about? What aspects of your
upbringing affected how you were as a
parent?

ALISON STIRLING

My dad died when I was 17 days old, and
there was my brother, 14 years older than
me, and then there were three stepchildren
and they were older as well, so, you know,

my mother had a lot to do. She needed money, so she went out and worked. So from an early age I was in the nursery, and then when I went to school that's when she said, 'Well, we'll get people in.' And I hated it. I absolutely hated it. And she was trying her absolute best but it got to the stage that she got me a blackboard. I wanted a bike but we couldn't afford one for Christmas so I got a blackboard.

IAIN STIRLING
Same letter. It's still a 'B', Alison. It begins with 'B'.

ALISON STIRLING
So I used to write notes to my mum on the blackboard, things that I would remember from school.

IAIN STIRLING
What, notes like you need to buy milk or like I learned that the sky is blue?

ALISON STIRLING
No, no. About something that happened that day – by the time she came in I might have forgotten about it. So I would write that

down and then my mother would write
something on the blackboard and it became a
wee thing with us, and it was great. But it
doesn't beat coming in to your mum and
saying, 'You know what happened at school
today?' And then your nanna got ill. She got
cancer when I was 12 and that kind of turned
everything round. She had 18 months to live
and it turned her absolutely wild. So she
basically started giving things away because
she wanted things to be in order and it was
a hellish time to go through, and I realise
now that I was a carer, but at that point I
wouldn't have known I was. We got a new
washing machine and Mum couldn't use it – I
was doing it. So I think that's what made
me think I will never make my children old
before their time.

IAIN STIRLING
I mean, I'm 30 years old and still wouldn't
know how to use a dishwasher.

ALISON STIRLING
What is it you said to me when I said, 'Put
that in the washing machine'? You said, 'Is
that the one with the round door or the
square door?'

IAIN STIRLING
When was that?

ALISON STIRLING
You were in your teens.

IAIN STIRLING
I was easily in my teens. Oh my God.

A SHORT BIT OUTLINING HOW PARENTING HAS CHANGED

To help us understand how parenting has changed over the generations I'm going to use some terms to talk about each generation specifically. Once we're all on board with that code we can plough on with my hilarious content! The three main generations I'll be looking at are millennials (that's me), who roughly speaking were born between 1981 and 2002, Generation X (my parents' generation), who were born in the years 1961 to 1980, and finally baby boomers (my grandparents), who were born from 1941 to 1960. There, hopefully that'll save some time.

Parenting has seen massive shifts over the years. For me, the biggest affecting millennials is the shift from a fairly *laissez-faire* attitude towards a much more hands-on modern approach. Indeed, Generation X were known as the 'latch-door kids' because their baby-boomer folks were often out working or socialising, so the kids had to let themselves in when they went home after school or being out with their friends. Many Generation Xers lived with their parents in a manner more akin to flatmates than legal guardians. Take my mum, for example, communicating with her own mother through a blackboard like some sort of post-war WhatsApp messenger.

In fact in the 1980s parents' need to be away from their children and near their peers led to the construction of many age-restricted communities where adults could hang out in child-free zones, such as holiday resorts, and the rise of the infamous 'kids clubs' that are still popular to this day. Parents could go lie on a sun lounger while their kid was taken off to play with some out-of-work actor in his mid-twenties dressed like a clown or a prince (royalty, not the pop star). To many this might sound like sloppy parenting, but I bet it sounds like heaven to the modern kid who constantly has to keep their parents updated on their movements via their mobile phone, or can't post anything online because they know their parents have set up secret online accounts just so they can keep an eye on their comings and goings. Want to go to the cinema on your own? Of course you can! Well, I mean, Mum and Dad will be there, obviously, but they'll sit a few rows back.

KIDS ARE SHIT AT STUFF

On the face of things it would seem that this overprotection is born out of a parent's need to protect and serve their precious little ones. But I mean, how can I, or any millennial for that matter, hope to embrace adult life when Mummy and Daddy are still willing to do your washing when you're well into your thirties? In fact, after the podcast was recorded with my mum, she made us mac and cheese while I was on my phone.

But a sort of misplaced love isn't the only factor at work here. Although it is an undisputed fact that children are beautiful and fragile presents from God that need to be protected and nurtured, there is no getting away from the truth that they take fucking ages to do stuff. Watching a child getting dressed (and please only do so if the appropriate social and legal norms are in place) is one of the most excruciating processes in the history of mankind. They don't know which hole to stick their head through in a T shirt, socks are approached with a level of concentration that should be reserved for bomb-disposal experts and you can dream on if you think these dafties are getting anything on their person should that garment involve buttons. So at the end of the day it is much easier for Mum and Dad to dress the dithering idiot themselves, thus saving an invaluable half an hour. This time can then be spent doing fun 'parent' things like not sleeping or wishing you still had disposable income.

If any of you question whether or not parents dress their children out of love or necessity, simply watch a mother putting shoes on her toddler. It remains one of the most barbaric acts I have ever seen performed by one human on another. And I say that as a man who's spent two long weekends on lads' holidays to Amsterdam. Viciously smashing Thomas the Tank Engine strap-ups onto the soles of unsuspecting three-year-olds is not the action of someone in love, but rather of a women who is 20 minutes late for a swimming lesson.

This same notion applies to all aspects of life. You name it, kids are shit at it: setting the table, taking in the washing, doing homework. All activities can be sped up tenfold by simply doing them yourself. But this 'overprotection' comes at a price. Millennials are growing up not learning necessary life skills that will help them function in the real world and that will help them move out and go on to live their own independent adult lives.

Similarly parents can find solace through constantly caring for their offspring and this can cause them to turn into someone who not only creates a reliance on their services but craves it – the 'devouring mother'. Having served others for so long she becomes obsessive, controlling and even violently scared of the idea of being alone. Mum might complain about my dirty pants and constant iPhone antics, but what would she do without me?

Disney films always manage to capture this idea brilliantly, whether it be the Evil Queen in *Snow White* or Ursula in *The Little Mermaid*. The lengths to which the devouring mother will go to maintain control over those that once relied on them are not to be underestimated. Admittedly the actions of our Disney characters aren't *exactly* the same sort of thing you see happening as a result of a Gen Xer's over-parenting, but to be fair to Walt (Disney) I think we can all agree that *The Little Mermaid* wouldn't be nearly as good a film if Ursula's evil deed was agreeing to pick Ariel up from the bus stop every day after school because she didn't like the walk ... sorry, the swim. If Ariel had been walking she wouldn't have wanted picking up – that girl bloody loved a good wander!

As children begin to rely on their parents more and more to give them assistance through life, so parents begin to rely on their children to give them purpose to theirs. This cycle can lead to children not leaving home until much later in life. It is mutually beneficial for both parties so long as life is preferable 'in the parental home' or 'under the sea', depending on what literature you've read on the subject. And then there are several changing social factors:

- A rise in house prices means children don't move out until later in life.
- Parents are having fewer children, so that each child gets more attention.
- Parents are having kids older, when they're more settled, so are more likely to stay in with their kids than go out and socialise.
- An increased focus and pressure on giving children the correct moral compass.

Parenthood is something I think about more and more as I get older because for some unknown reason my friends keep insisting on having bloody kids. Making babies, on purpose. How adult is that? 'OK, babe, I'm going to start leaving it in.' I mean, they possibly put it in a slightly more romantic way, but you get the idea.

As a comedian who is forever trying to rid himself of his dreaded ego, other people's children can be a real stumbling block on my path to enlightenment. Mainly due to the fact that most of my friends seem to like their children more than they like me. Me! How long have you known your kid? Like a couple of weeks? We've been friends since freshers' week, you ungrateful bastard. What has your kid ever done for you? Every day you have to tell that thing to stop crying, wipe its bum and put it to bed. You've only had to do that for me twice. It was my birthday and you had given me a bottle of rum as a present – in many ways you only had yourself to blame. I mean, this shouldn't even be a competition. Your baby can't talk, I'm the voice of *Love Island*. I'm objectively better. That baby has never 'cued the text' or 'paged Dr Marcel'. I should be top of your list all day, every day.

I guess I just question anyone who can feel something so strong towards someone who's done so little. I know I'm a Liverpool fan and will follow them wherever they go despite a relative dry patch, trophy-wise, over recent seasons, but boy do they play good football and Jürgen Klopp is a total BABE. Seriously, even if you aren't a footy fan you need to check out my main man Jürgen. The guy is like the dad you've always wanted. I mean, who wouldn't want a dad called Jürgen? Am I right? Even if, like me, you have an incredible father who would quite literally lie down in traffic for you, a day spent watching Jürgen stare out the opposition from the halfway line while they do their pre-match warm-up is one of the most heroic pieces of needlessly alpha behaviour you will ever see. Try not to whisper 'Daddy' under your breath while he does it. I dare ya!

So while Liverpool can reward my love and loyalty even in the absence of any silverware, what can your baby do? It can't even talk! The thing could be a prick. We don't know yet. Half the people in the world are pricks so it's statistically likely that your baby is an arsehole. It hasn't even expressed a view. I mean, it could be a racist baby. You don't know. It is bald and white, so it's already got the uniform.

THE RACE TO ADULTHOOD

I used to dread the idea of getting older. There, I said it, I'm getting older. As much as it pains me to admit, the inevitable passage of time is slowly catching up on me. Hangovers are, not necessarily becoming physically worse, but the sadness that I feel the day after is really increasing – the dreaded 'beer fear' is getting more and more intense as I start to wizen with age. It'll take more than a Lucozade and some screaming into the shower head to abolish that voice in my head asking, 'What the hell are you doing with your life?' In my early twenties the voice was a gentle whisper that I could ignore; when I hit 29 it bought a megaphone.

Older. Like, who would want that? More responsibility, more stress and more wrinkles. For us millennials the dawning of adulthood can be a real point of stress. We've grown up in a world where perfection is pitched as a realistic goal, a thing to be achieved as opposed to some sort of abstract concept to be aimed for but never quite reached. Because perfection is impossible, like not looking a total prick in a vest top or trying to sound interesting when talking about bitcoin.

Not only do we see adulthood as this part in our lives when we live in complete and utter bliss with all our shit together, but there seems to be a massive stress for my generation to get to that stage in life as quick as possible, with no slip-ups on the way. I mean, what would be the point in owning a beautiful new sports car when you're too old and grey to absolutely smash the likes on Insta? I find it hilarious when an older person buys a fancy new sports car and is accused of having a mid-life crisis. Really? Are they having a crisis or just earning enough money now to be able to afford one?

The pressure is on. You're getting old, and you need to sort *everything* out before you get there. If you are feeling like that right now I'm here to tell you it's OK. If you're reading this and panicking that you're never going to win an award, make a million pounds or even run that company, then take a deep breath. Everyone is panicking, about everything, all the time. As you get older you learn one thing for sure. No one has a fucking clue what the hell they're doing. Your mates don't know what the hell they're doing with their lives, your parents had no clue what they were doing when they brought you up – hell, even the President of the United States is just a big clueless mess guessing his way through life. Although that has become more and more horribly apparent in recent years.

In a recent chat with Spencer Owen, AKA Spencer FC, a brilliant content creator with over a million subscribers on YouTube, he spoke very eloquently about why he is glad success has come to him slightly later in life (by YouTube standards) and why too much, too soon can actually impact negatively on your life in the long-term. We started by discussing how hard it must be for pop stars who achieve success early on, which then fades.

Interview with Spencer Owen –
'Someone asks you for a cup of tea. No thanks, I've been to the moon'

IAIN STIRLING

I look at some pop stars who are, like, private jets to LA, living the life, blah-di-blah. And maybe they didn't save like they should have done. And they're 24 …

BAD PARENTING

SPENCER OWEN

Yeah, what do you from there? It's like that
Buzz Aldrin thing: you've gone to the moon
and someone asks you for a cup of tea. No
thanks, I've been to the moon.

IAIN STIRLING

I've been to the moon. What do you do?

SPENCER OWEN

I've had moments. I've been amazingly
privileged to have played football in front
of crowds of 20,000 and 30,000 people
multiple times, which I never thought I'd
say. And they're amazing moments. The last
Wembley Cup, I played in front of 34,000
people. I've put on that whole event – that
was my baby. Huge success. Within an hour
of the game finishing I'm sort of sitting
there thinking, 'What do I? What's next?'
And you hear from World Cup winners – a much
higher level. They win a World Cup, have
half an hour of elation and 'Oh my God, this
is so good.' And then suddenly you're
thinking I've just completed the one thing
I had in my life driving me. So I think that
it's really important to stress that it's
not going to solve your problems. If you've

got problems you need to deal with them wherever you are, whatever you do. I think that so many guys I talk to behind the scenes, hugely popular YouTubers with many more subscribers than I have, making crazy, crazy money, to the outside world have got everything they could possibly need. But they've just got no motivation. And you hit a point where you think, 'So what am I doing it for?'

IAIN STIRLING
I mean, if you're 20 and you're jet-skiing in the Caribbean and have a massive big house, that's cool, but what do you do when you're … what do you when you're 30 or 31?

SPENCER OWEN
I'm pretty confident that you weren't, at the age of 5 or 6 or 10 or 15, saying, 'I want to be a stand-up because I want to have a big house.'

IAIN STIRLING
I didn't know it was a thing.

SPENCER OWEN
You wanted to do stand-up.

40

IAIN STIRLING

But also because of my background I never knew that stand-up was … I mean, I knew there were Billy Connolly and Lee Evans and they were superstars, but I didn't know you could make a living doing what I do. I did a show in Birmingham, 400 people, sold out the room, and I couldn't believe it. I'm delighted with that. But if I was selling out the Birmingham Glee on my own tour when I was 22, I'd want to be at Wembley now. You'd drive yourself insane. That's why I've enjoyed it, but I'm glad I've done uni and even the kids' TV thing. It was a bit of fame but it's not mad.

SPENCER OWEN

Yeah. You also learned the trade in so many ways.

IAIN STIRLING

Yeah. A central London club isn't letting the guy that talks to a puppet dog in for free to a table with a bottle of vodka, and I'm not getting paid enough money to pay for it myself so I'm not going to those places. But then it comes when I'm 28 and I'm like, 'Oh, it's too loud, I want a seat.'

SPENCER OWEN

It's the same with me. I get a load of plaudits from people, from parents saying they like my channel for their kids or whatever. It's not that it's something that deserves praise, it's just that if I was doing what I do now at 18, I wouldn't be making those rubbish videos probably, because I made those videos and no one watched them. I didn't make videos filming a guy committing suicide in a forest, so, as a moral barometer, I'm certainly not at that level of it. But when we're younger we do make mistakes. And a lot of the other YouTubers have never done anything that bad, but they've still made silly videos. I would have done it too. It's just I never really knew what I wanted to do. Now I have ideas and there's other things I'd like to go and try to do, but it was only when I was like 23, 24, maybe even 25, and I left full-time employment and deliberately said, 'Right, I'm going to try and do this.' Most of the YouTubers aren't even that age yet. So how can they expect to know these answers? I remember sitting down with my dad when I finished uni, and I actually said to him, 'What advice can you give me?'

BAD PARENTING

IAIN STIRLING

If I had said that to my daddy he would have crumbled.

SPENCER OWEN

I remember him saying something quite boring – take your time, find what you want to do, don't rush into anything, don't rush into getting married, don't rush into settling down, don't rush into living in one place or doing one job. Just take your time, which was quite valuable in many ways. So I went and tried things. I did things I didn't like, I did loads of jobs I didn't like, some of which were rubbish jobs, some of which were actually good jobs, but I didn't like them.

IAIN STIRLING

And that's another problem with this social-media thing. It's not just footballers or YouTubers, now everyone succeeds so young. You go and watch something like *Britain's Got Talent*, and there's a 17-year-old saying, 'This is my last shot now.' What you are talking about? You're 17. You've got a young person's railcard for another 10 years. You're fine. The rush to get there

almost comes down to that Instagram thing
of 'What's the point in winning an Oscar
when you're 40 because you won't even look
good in a selfie?'

SPENCER OWEN
I'd much rather win an Oscar at 60.

IAIN STIRLING
Oh, mate.

SPENCER OWEN
Cos if you win it at 20 you've been to the
moon. Where do you go?

AGE-WISE, WE'RE ALL IN THE 'SHIT BIT'

In the same way that Spencer had the support of his dad,
having a family around me is actually the main thing that has
saved me from the fear of growing old and becoming an adult
doomed to spend my life sitting on a couch in comfy slippers
while struggling to understand technology. I look at my family
at their different stages of life and realise that it's not all bad.
The beginning of life is great, we all know. Being properly
young, not having a care in the world and more importantly
having parents who are literally there to serve you from dawn

till dusk. They read books that you tell them to sing to you. Sing! Grown adults have to learn songs and perform them to you like you're a Roman emperor. A mini Roman emperor who could at any point shit himself.

Parents have a legal obligation to look after you, no matter what you do. That's mad if you think about it. At the age of three you could just go about sticking marbles up your bum and some fully grown adult would have to say, 'Well, I guess that's our day spent sorting out the marble situation, then.' If I had fully comprehended that notion as a kid I would have stuffed so much stuff up my bum at every possible occasion. 'It's pieces of Lego today, Dad. Forget the NHS, I think it'll be worth going private because this will be happening a lot. And if you do nothing, the courts will get involved!' For many millennials (particularly myself) this carries on long into your adult life. Well, maybe not the marbles thing – I've not done that in months now.

As great as being young is, there is a bit towards the end of life that I properly relish – being properly old, like nearly done, old. I can't wait to get to the stage when I can go out in public with my family, say something horrific and then just turn to them and say, 'Well, now that's your problem.' Go to the restaurant, scream something politically incorrect, turn to my son and say, 'You go deal with that and I'll stay here and finish off my Bolognese … I would probably tip the guy too – I was out of order!' I love old people like that. Just no one left to impress. No picture that they need to pose for to get likes on Instagram. No boss to answer to. They can do what they like, to who they like, when they like – so long as it doesn't involve too many stairs.

Despite all this freedom, however, what old people like to do is gardening and when they like to do it is 6 a.m. What is it with old people and getting up early? I know they say the early bird catches the worm but not when that bird has a Zimmer frame. Have a lie-in! What have you got to do that's so urgent? 'I need to send a letter.' A letter? Do it in the afternoon or just don't send a letter! Text your friend Karen and then press the snooze button. 'Karen doesn't know how to work her phone.' OK, fine. Well, 6 a.m. it is then. Even if they do have an obsession with early rises and mundane tasks, there is still a madness that surrounds all pensioners, and for reasons that I believe become more clear as you read this book, I am so very drawn to it.

My gran was like that. Wonderful woman, all six foot two of her. Now, her height isn't relevant to the narrative in any way whatsoever, but I think we'll all agree it's a lovely visual image to carry through this chapter – a tall, crazy, old, female version of me. Imagine me but taller, with a fetching grey perm – you are all very welcome. She wasn't tied down by the rules of society; she didn't have to go to dinner parties and pretend to be fine with the very obvious fact that Colin was getting way too much attention. Fuck you, Colin, you're only three weeks old and already you're pissing me off. As a little aside I got my friend to read this paragraph back for me just to see if perhaps me imagining my own gran telling a three-week-old infant to 'fuck off' was too harsh, especially given my previous in this area, and my friend simply replied: 'Who the fuck calls their baby Colin?'

Anywho, the point is I always admired my gran's general disregard for 'the rules'. Sometimes it was adorable, such as the time she assumed that Postman Pat tinned spaghetti shapes were all shaped like different post offices in her local area, and sometimes it was funny in retrospect, like watching my mum chase Gran's 1970 black Ford Fiesta down the street after Gran had kindly accepted my and my little sister's request to 'get driven to the shops in the boot'. That is panic. The point is she was bloody marvellous. Awful driver, though, but still – six foot two.

THE ANTIGUA FUCK-UP (PART I)

One of my fondest memories of my gran was around the time of my first break-up. My family and I were on holiday in Antigua. I was comfortably in my twenties. Some of you might think that's weird, and I guess in some respects it was. I had my reasons, primarily the nasty break-up and being a mollycoddled millennial. My mother still felt the responsibility was solely on her shoulders to make sure her 'little boy's' broken heart was mended. Oh, fuck off, Freud!

You never really forget that first break-up. It never leaves, always there in the back of your mind, incurable, sort of like the sadness version of herpes. Mums are the only people that can really help, in my experience. My mum, I mean. I'm not just roaming the streets screaming, 'She left me!' at any woman with a buggy. I tried to talk to my friends about it – that was a bloody disaster. They just stare at you helplessly, a blank expression etched onto their faces, like when someone's farted in a lift and everyone is trying to look like it wasn't them that did it. I mean, I couldn't move for messages on Facebook and Twitter hoping I was all right and 'if I needed anything just ask'. Now, I'm not saying those people's concerns weren't genuine, but I will say that, although undoubtedly worried for my well-being, they certainly weren't willing to travel in order to demonstrate it. There *was* someone who would, however. Someone who would move mountains for her 'little boy', her little 26-year-old, mortgage-owning, law-degree-having little boy – Mummy.

So I'm on this holiday, and I'm fine, totally fine, don't look at me like that, I'm fine. We were three days in to 'the big holi-day', and unlike our Scottish holidays of old there wasn't a caravan in sight; however, exactly like our Scottish holidays of old, there was rain ... and lots of it. Nothing gets a mum down more than rain on the main holiday. They obsess over it, constantly mentioning home. 'In Scotland it's beautiful,' Mum would remark while staring out the hotel window at the grey antigen sky, like a convict looking out through his cell bars. 'Three days' rain on the main holiday. I can't believe it. I'm going to call Thomsons.' Yeah, Mum, you do that. I'm sure there is some policy that covers entirely uncontrollable and unprecedented Caribbean drizzle. They'll give us a full refund

– they can claim the costs back from Mother Nature's insurance policy.

In order to alleviate some of the pent-up cabin (relatively upmarket hotel) fever we decided to go on a family drive. Is there anything more relaxing than a family drive? Mum shouting at Dad for driving too close to one side of the road, Dad not speaking to Mum because it wasn't until two hours into the drive she realised the map was the wrong way round, while the kids in the back are relentless with their constant stream of 'Are we there yet?' and 'Iain pulled my hair again', which for the record was an absolute fucking lie. The only person totally at peace in this tin can of pent-up passive–aggressive anger was my gran, who just sat in the middle seat knitting. Not a worry in the world. Just absolutely over the moon to be out the house.

We drove on some more until we came to a red light, barely visible as the thick rain lashed down all around. My dad nearly missed the light, slamming on the brakes just in time and skidding to a stop as my mother muttered something loving under her breath about him being a 'homicidal maniac', and then we waited. What a holiday this was shaping up to be. I should get the selfie stick out right now!

After a few seconds I noticed a huge Antiguan man walking alongside the car. Now Antigua isn't one for pavements and all that boring infrastructure stuff, and why not, it's a paradise. You don't need pavements in paradise. We all know what happened to paradise when they put up a parking lot so I was delighted that Antigua had decided to keep things simple. While we waited patiently for the lights to change, this behemoth of a man was now sludging his way through the grassy knoll that ran adjacent to the road. Eventually he stopped, almost parallel to our vehicle, and started to fiddle with his belt.

Now the next 30 seconds of my life are etched into my psyche in such detail I don't think the images will ever leave me. I could be on my death bed, surrounded by loved ones, adoring fans, my wife and kids staring into my dimming eyes, and as they all ask me, in perfect unison, 'What are your dying words, our beloved?' I will whisper with my final breath, 'Once, in Antigua, me and my mum spent 30 seconds staring at the same stranger's penis ... Oh, and I once told an eight-year-old to go fuck himself.'

Our Antiguan man-mountain of a friend had decided to remove his aforementioned penis – from his shorts, not physically from his body; he didn't rip it off, stick it in a jar and hand it to my beloved mother – he simply popped it out his pants and started having a widdle in the street. So as a man peed in the middle of the afternoon in the middle of the road, the Stirling family stared on. Mother seemed furious that yet more unwanted drizzle had affected our main holiday. I was paralysed with fear – 'paralysed by the penis', if you will. Someone had to do something, but who was it going to be?

'WHAT DO YOU WANT TO BE WHEN YOU GROW UP?' I'VE NO IDEA, MATE. I'M ONLY SEVEN.

It's weird the first time you find yourself in a situation in which you feel like you need to protect your parents. The role reversal is a real rite of passage into adulthood. That first time your dad can't pick up a particularly heavy box or needs consoling following the loss of a pet, or when your mum is left helplessly staring at a stranger's penis. Having these figures of strength and unconditional love turn to you for help and showing they're not infallible – nothing makes you feel more like a grown-up. Like the first time you cross a road before the green man comes on and you notice those around you follow you on your journey to the other side of the road. I've never felt more powerful in my life. Why did the chicken cross the road? Because Iain Stirling is a fucking alpha male!

The reason this role reversal hit me particularly hard was in no little part down to the fact that when it comes to my own parents I am a textbook millennial. My parents have always put my hopes and desires above their own at any cost. Evenings were spent taking me to any club or hobby that remotely tick-led my fancy. Football, tennis, golf, swimming, boy scouts, amateur dramatics – you name it, I was painfully average at all of them, but Christ was I diverse. In theatre, people speak of the 'triple threat', one of those talented son of a guns that could sing, dance and act. Well, I, Iain Stirling, was more like an sexuple threat. I would sing, dance and act, while in a swimming pool, playing golf with Akela looking on, ready to give me my putting badge. This severely watered down my ability to excel in any particular area, but I was having a lovely time and Mummy said I was good, so what does actual objective success even matter? As I type this I can imagine my mum saying to me, 'You weren't average at all, son. You were uniquely talented.'

Every problem I ever faced was never faced alone. I always had the support of my loving parents no matter what. And when it came to her baby boy there were few lengths my mother wouldn't go to. When I got bullied, my mum didn't just go into the school. She didn't just tell me that I should ignore it. What Alison Stirling did was sign me up to self-defence classes three times a week. She had to buy me all the gear, drive me there and back in the evenings and give up her weekends for competitions and exams – all because of that one time Gavin pushed me in a puddle.

Now I'm not saying all my mother's acts of parenting were needlessly overbearing. Self-defence is undoubtedly a useful skill, and the weekly socialising and exercise were great for my physical and mental health. The issue I have is with the discipline Mother decided for me – judo. The problem was that judo didn't have any real-life implications in terms of thwarting those evil bullies (well, Gavin). As a martial art it is definitely one of the more passive disciplines. On the intimidation scale I was less Conor McGregor and more Gandhi. First of all, for judo to work you and your opponent need to be in a hold, and secondly for that hold to work you both need to be wearing the appropriate gown. 'Oh, you want my lunch money, do you? Well, stick on this dressing gown because we're about to cuddle.' I carried on with judo for a further seven years, until a little girl called Katie snapped my collarbone and, as a family, we decided I should maybe focus on the arts. During those seven years the bullying never subsided, but my health improved significantly, so it wasn't a complete waste of time. I imagine Gavin is now a professional internet troll.

Although it seems like a great thing for millennials to grow up with parents willing to go above and beyond in order for them to live the best lives possible, some experts have spoken out, claiming millennials have grown up with what is now being regarded as 'bad parenting'. This phrase might make it sound like we all grew up with some sort of abuse or neglect, but actually it's quite the opposite. 'Bad parenting' is the idea that our parents told us throughout our childhoods that we were special and could achieve anything we wanted, so long as we wanted it badly enough. During my childhood I remember my mum constantly telling me that I was 'special' and could 'achieve anything'.

Other ultimately useless information was also thrown at me on regular occasions, such as 'Iain, the bullies are picking on you because they're jealous.' Yeah, that's right, Mum, the bullies are jealous of my stutter and my lazy eye. The truth is that kids pick on kids because kids are pricks and picking on people is fun. It's called 'making fun' for a reason. Sometimes as a child you need to be told about the harsh realities of life, which I was protected from my entire childhood. I was never told about failure growing up; I was constantly protected from it. I don't think I went to a funeral until I was at university. Heaven forbid I would be made aware of the fact that all people eventually die. I wasn't ready for that. I was only 20.

As well as limiting our exposure to the harsh realities of life, our parents would also go above and beyond to ensure our dreams and desires could be realised. Millennial kids were never brought up with a belief that they were flawed or that they had to be realistic in their dreams. Yet despite this increased protection and support, millennials are still overall a lot less happy than their Gen X parents. How can this be? The answer is in our increased life expectations, dreams that were far ahead of anything Gen X parents ever hoped for. Essential happiness comes down to a very simple formula.

HAPPINESS = REALITIES - EXPECTATIONS

It makes total sense if you think about it. Your happiness is essentially the current situation you find yourself in, less what you expected your life to be like. This is the mistake many parents have made. Tell your kid they will grow up to be an astronaut and, shock horror, a reliable, well-paid job in admin will never really live up to their childhood expectations. This is not to say a child's dreams shouldn't be nurtured and encouraged, but you also need to teach them about the world's harsh realities to temper expectations. I asked my mum whether she felt any pressure to monitor my expectations when I first started in comedy.

IAIN STIRLING

I'm at university. I'm studying law but I clearly want to be a comedian, which in our family is not a thing you do.

ALISON STIRLING

No.

IAIN STIRLING

Is there a worry like, 'Well, I want to encourage him and make him do well, but if this idiot keeps doing gigs above pubs to six people for the rest of his life …'?

ALISON STIRLING

Do you know what, I can honestly say, 'No.' Your sister wanted to dance and the school made a big thing of it and said, 'You're surely going to discourage her.' And I said, 'There is absolutely no way I would discourage this.' And I, hand on heart, wanted you to do what you wanted to, because my mother banged on about how she wanted me to be a hairdresser. She was going to buy a shop and I would do hair, and she would tell everybody. And it got to such a stage that I dreaded the time to leave school because I thought I'm going to have to tell her, but she would just think it was just a phase I was going through and all of a sudden I would want to do hair.

IAIN STIRLING
And the weirdest thing about it is she's doing all that because she wants you to do well, do you know what I mean?

ALISON STIRLING
I think she just thought that this is something she could do for me, so instead of asking, instead of letting me find what I wanted to do, it was just, 'This is the thing.' And I remember I would go through hoops to try not to hurt her in any way by saying, 'There is not a hope in hell that I will ever be a hairdresser.'

IAIN STIRLING
I'm never doing a blue rinse in my life.

ALISON STIRLING
I could not. I'm not artistic and the thought of standing with somebody's hair and doing something with that, no. It just was not on the cards for me. That was never going to happen, so I think I realised from

an early age that you're going to get on so
much further if you do what you want to do.
If you make the wrong decision, it's your
decision. You do it.

IAIN STIRLING
Yeah.

ALISON STIRLING
If somebody else makes the decision it's so
easy to then say, and I've heard all this
with friends, 'Oh, my parents made me do
this.' And what they get is not a chip on
their shoulder - it's a boulder. So your
doing comedy was absolutely not an issue.
People in the law school would say, 'Oh, for
goodness sake, why is he not doing this?'

IAIN STIRLING
Because he thinks it's the most boring thing
that's ever happened in his entire life.

ALISON STIRLING
Yeah, or they'd say, 'You'll be
disappointed,' and I'm going, 'No, I would
never be disappointed,' because part of me
knows that if you wanted to do it, you would
apply yourself because that's what you chose

to do and, to be fair, when you did your first sketch at school, I mean, you just loved it. You came alive in that. You never came alive in law school.

IAIN STIRLING

As you know I studied with very, very clever men, in that they all went on to do amazing things - Samoa, Hong Kong, they've been everywhere with the law. They'd go and speak to the dissertation adviser and all that, and it wasn't that I was lazy and didn't do it. It just never dawned on me that it was an option because I was never that into it. So I was trying really hard, but I think the thing about being passionate about something is that you're going to work hard at it by default because you're thinking about it all the time.

ALISON STIRLING

Exactly.

IAIN STIRLING

Like even if I go out and get absolutely hammered, and it happens more often than it should, I'll lie in in the morning and write a funny bit of stand-up. Well, not

even write it, I'll just think it and I'll
have a thing for stand-up so I've done work
that morning, whereas with law I didn't
like it. So I had to drag myself into that
library and force my way through all those
books. So I was not as good at it just
because I wasn't into it.

ALISON STIRLING
And I think that's the thing. I've
definitely learned that from Mum. When I
didn't go into hairdressing there had to be
these excuses because she'd told so many
people, and I did fine. Like you, I applied
myself in what I wanted to and I did well
and that's fine. I wouldn't have done well
in the hairdressers. I would have been
absolutely miserable.

IAIN STIRLING
You would have hated it.

ALISON STIRLING
I would have hated it. Well, you never know,
I might not have.

IAIN STIRLING

You'd be good at chatting to people, the people bit.

ALISON STIRLING

Yeah, the chat is one thing. But what about the haircut?

IAIN STIRLING

Well, I had a lovely chat but I've not got an ear. Apart from that …

ALISON STIRLING

And the hair. I'm not sure what this is supposed to be.

THE ANTIGUA FUCK-UP (PART II)

So, back in Antigua, the whole Stirling clan are staring at a stranger's ding-dong. Like an X-rated *Gogglebox*. I'd say everyone was watching on in horror, but that isn't actually true. Mother was doing that classic middle-class British thing of just pretending that the horrific event unfolding five feet from her head wasn't happening. It's a real British talent, acting completely indifferent as horror unfolds all around. So as this man urinated next to Gran, Mother started showing the family the many interesting functions of the rental car: 'Oh, look, you press this button and the lights come on. The CD goes in and if you press here it comes straight back out.'

I, as the son and the man I was slowly becoming, failed in my challenge to step up and deal with the situation myself. So it fell to Gran. After a long pause and a few more buttons pressed by Mum, my gran declared loudly: 'Look how black it is.'

Now, for the record, I am fully aware that this is a totally unacceptable, offensive thing to say. And everyone was offended by the statement – except me. Because I wasn't looking at the guy outside our rental car; I was looking at my gran, who wasn't looking at the man either. She was staring out the opposite side of the car, into the sky, at a massive rain cloud. This gave me the opportunity to finally save my family. I wasn't an alpha who could take control – I had been too mollycoddled by my loving parents to take any action that didn't involve their direct support and encouragement – but what I could do was be funny. So, with my parents still in utter shock and disgust at the situation that was unfolding, I said: 'Hey Nanna, want to stand underneath it and I'll get a photo?'

My gran's reply was almost instant: 'Pass me my umbrella.'

At which point Mum just panicked and shot off. She went from awkward Brit abroad to bank-job getaway driver in two sentences. It was a beautiful thing to watch as my mum sliced through the thick drizzle (from the clouds, not the penis), jumping red lights like she was trying to drive away from her own shame and embarrassment. It'll not work, Mum, because Gran's in the back. After a minute or so, and with my parents still totally oblivious to the whole cloud situation, my gran said: 'I've not seen one that big since your grandad passed away.'

What a lovely moment. God bless you, Nanna.

CHAPTER 2

SCHOOLED

'The Best Days of Your Life ...'

School years, love them or hate them, one thing is for sure: they will leave an indelible mark on your psyche that takes a fair bit to shift. Doesn't matter if it's the jock that never quite grew up and accepted that after school no one gives a flying fuck about you having captained the football team that got to the semi-finals of the Scottish schools cup or that once you got to second base with the prom queen. Or the poor bastard that spent his life getting picked on by cowards who were just glad it wasn't them receiving twice-daily beatings and now spends his days locked in his room playing video games. Now I'm neither of those two extreme cases, but if I had to sit myself somewhere on that spectrum I would much rather be spending my evening chatting over my Turtle Beach headset while playing *Fortnite* online with my gamer friends than with 'Jimbo' and 'the lads from his golf club'. You know the type, those guys that seem to punctuate every sentence with 'WHAYs!' and 'OI OIs!' Now, although the guttural screams are relatively difficult to portray using the written word, I'm sure you can remember a time you've heard those alpha tones fill your local town centre like a group of Burberry-clad wolves howling into the midnight sky. I remember once hearing a guy in baggy black jeans and an Alexisonfire T-shirt describe them as 'a load of coked-up Teletubbies'. I liked that. I liked that a lot.

It's not that the alpha-male night out can't have moments of genuine hilarity. These lads can get it spot on – on occasion. I was once out in Glasgow after a gig. I love gigging in Glasgow; Glaswegians are the perfect mix of attentive and mental. That's what you want from an audience. People often, and mistakenly, think a good audience is one that gets involved and keeps the comedian on their toes. Every interview I've ever done has always had the dreaded question, 'What's the best heckle you've ever received?' The truth being that there isn't one. No heckle is ever good. Normally it's just some drunk twat screaming incoherently because the town they were born in or a football team they vaguely recognise was mentioned. You want an audience that'll sit there and just get into it, and let the comic get on with their job. But if the comic does ask a member of the audience a question then we want something we can work with. And if you want a mad answer then Glasgow is the place for you.

Anyway, I was in this pub in Glasgow, in the toilets if you really want me to hit you with specifics in front of the urinal, reading a poster I'm sure must have been about van hire or Viagra. By the way, any girls reading this who haven't experienced the joys of the gents' toilets, they are often covered in posters advertising things men can't do after a few pints, namely drive or get an erection. To be fair to the Viagra marketing team, it is excellent targeting. What better place to reach out to people who have penises and inadequate sex lives than the gents' toilet of a Wetherspoons?

On this occasion I was distracted from looking at the picture of a man with a hat balancing on his shaft, as well as the great deals I could get on a Fiat Fiorino, by something amazing behind me at the sink. A man was tipping his head right back, almost like he was trying to limbo underneath the taps. My first reaction was obviously this man is off his face on drugs. I mean literally off his face. It looked like he was trying to scratch his own eyes out. Now we've all been there in the past: gone to a pub, got too drunk, retired to the bathroom, caught your own reflection in the pub mirror and had to have a quiet word with yourself. 'What are you doing with your life, mate? You're hammered in a Wetherspoons on a Tuesday!'

But this guy must have been so aghast with what he had seen in the mirror that he was starting to claw at his own head. In order to get a better look I finished up, noted down the number of what seemed like a really good Fiat dealership and moved towards the sink – the whole time trying to catch a glimpse of what my battered friend was actually doing. After a few seconds I could see that he was trying to get his contact lenses in. Now, I've only used contact lenses a few times, but in my limited experience the two most important factors are having a steady hand and a sterile environment. I didn't think the best time to insert tiny shards of glass into your eyes would be when you're absolutely hammered in a public toilet in Glasgow. But, fair play to this lad, he absolutely smashed it. He popped them straight in. It was actually really impressive to watch, like when someone throws rubbish in a bin, first time, from distance, or when someone recites the entire *Fresh Prince of Bel-Air* rap perfectly, including that weird third verse that no one's ever heard before. A man that could barely stand managed to insert tiny little windows over his retinas – fair play, lad.

The only issue now was that I had become totally transfixed by the guy – I could no longer take my eyes off the dude. Do you know that horrible moment when you're staring at someone but have no real knowledge that you're doing it? They then catch your eye, and you can try to look away but the damage is already done. The only thing worse is when you try to get a photo of someone on the sly on public transport. Nothing malicious, they just look like a friend, have a classic retro football shirt on or have a really cool moustache. You just want a little photo to stick in a WhatsApp group. But as you go to take the snap, when it's too late to turn back you realise the flash is on. There is no getting out of that very public clusterfuck, even if you say to the guy in question: 'Sorry, mate, I just really like your moustache.'

Back in the toilet our very drunk friend had caught me hook, line and sinker. He walked towards me, squinting to try to get me into focus, his eyes still clearly adjusting to the lenses. I was frozen. What was going to happen next? What if he killed me? What would the police tell my mum?

'Officer, put me out my misery and just tell me. How did he die?'

'Well, he stared at a complete stranger in a public toilet.'

This wasn't how I wanted to go out. Not like this, not in a Wetherspoons. If you are going to take me out, at least take me next door to the All Bar One – even a Revolution bar would be preferable. While these irrelevant and completely useless thoughts ran riot through my brain, the man continued to advance towards me, the squinting lessening as I came more and more into focus. What happened next is a perfect example of why you should never judge anyone. Just because they're hammered in a Wetherspoons doesn't mean they punch anyone that stares at them for an uncomfortable amount of time. Sometimes they are comedy geniuses, and I'm not using that term lightly. That man stared into my face, his contact-lenses case now floating in the sink and simply declared: 'Mate, you look 3D as fuck!'

Then off he went to rejoin his mate, oblivious to the relief and delight that now flooded through my system. These alpha-male, former school-football captains can be funny as hell, but I still wouldn't spend an evening with the nutters. I've never understood those guys that 'hit the town' wearing near enough matching shirts and identical dark jeans (which are ripped, obviously, because these crazy katz are rule breakers – rule breakers who shop exclusively from Topman) to go 'on the pull'. I don't know what the logic is there – what are they hoping will happen? That seven girls will walk in, all looking for the exact same guy? Statistically, lads, that is incredibly unlikely, but don't worry if Snow White and her seven dumbos fail to show, you can always just go off and punch something. Or have a kebab. Or both. Lovely stuff.

Anyway, the point I'm making is that school relationships can leave scars that may stick with you long into your adult years, and maybe even filter from your subconscious onto the pages of your first book. I'm guessing.

IF YOU REALLY THINK ABOUT IT, SCHOOL IS INSANE

School is obviously a very necessary part of any child's development and a major step on the way to adulthood, but I can't help but find the artifice of the whole thing unimaginably hilarious. I mean, you lock a load of children in a building, children who have nothing in common other than the area in which they grew up. Seventeen-year-olds on the precipice of adulthood share lunch halls, and normally over-cooked baked potatoes, with twelve-years-olds who are still dealing with the brutal impact of puberty. And the whole thing is overseen by some random fifty-year-old that no one actually knows in any sort of detail at all. 'Head teacher', I believe they are called. But who is this person and why do they require this level of power over children? All you know is that when a child is really naughty they get sent to that dictator's office and sometimes they never come back.

That's not to say I have anything against teachers. Quite the opposite. I think teaching is a very noble profession, one that is hugely underappreciated and underpaid, in my humble opinion. Ohhhh, Jeremy Corbyn, down with the Tories, etc. However, I just don't understand the logic of a school child who decides they want to go into the teaching profession. When I was at school my mind constantly wondered at the things I wanted to do and be when I grew older: fireman, vet, footballer and that one weird week when I decided I wanted to be a break dancer. I took lessons, even bought a doo-rag, and there isn't a day goes by that I don't regret it. We were taught by a lovely man called Craig, who would constantly tell us how the noble art of b-boying was dying, and the discipline was being taken over by gymnasts and acrobats. None of us had the heart to tell him we were all 14-year-old boys who were only on lesson 3 and just wanted to get good enough so we could kiss girls. It felt like that might have destroyed him.

So while I dreamt of single-handedly bringing b-boying back to its dancing roots, it would baffle me that there were some kids who dreamt of being a teacher. They would sit in a classroom and when asked, 'Where do you see yourself in 10 years' time?' they would reply, 'Still here, but facing the other way.' I'm not saying that is wrong. Please to God, if you're a teacher reading this, know that what you are doing is a hundred times more valuable to society than all my dick jokes put together. I just struggle to fully comprehend the logic. However, I am kind of jealous that you get to go in the staff room.

Nothing for me highlights the artificial nature of school more than when something goes wrong and the fragility of the school's structures and hierarchies are thrown into turmoil. One day you're all sitting there in the class, learning algebra because a man in his thirties told you to, then a child says those six words that have the whole fragile construct come crashing down: 'There's a dog in the playground!'

And that's when the mayhem starts. Children shoot from their seats and meld themselves against the school's single-glazing, all desperate to catch a glimpse of the mutt in question. Inevitably, the janitor is sent out to retrieve the confused hound with hilarious consequences. The once-intimidating, sour-faced old man who would unleash a stream of needlessly aggressive vitriol at even the cutest of pre-teens for dropping so much as a single chewing-gum wrapper is now chasing an Alsatian across the playing field like your wacky uncle after a few brandies at Christmas. Even the teacher's got their iPhone out and has started filming the whole thing on Snapchat (I would like to say that when I was at school, Snapchat was very much not a thing – thank Christ – but I'm just making myself seem more relevant for the youth, innit).

Now don't get me wrong, we've all seen dogs before, but not *in school*. It's the combination of dog and school that makes it magical. Like seeing a pigeon inside a restaurant or a former teacher at the pub quiz. They're two everyday things that shouldn't go together. Dogs don't come to school – this is a sacred place of learning. Or at least that's what the teachers want us to think. It's just one of those many moments when you realise school isn't some secure vacuum, there is no invisible force field separating us from the outside world – it's just a building. A building with a few more textbooks and dinner ladies than anyone would normally expect. The whole thing is a construct.

These moments are not just limited to a rogue canine on the football pitch. Everyone has had that bizarre moment in school when you get into class and sit down to notice a hushed silence, a weird, awkward atmosphere, then it strikes you. This class has no teacher in it. I remember my first high-school teacherless class. The primal vibes running through that room were palpable. In that moment it feels like *Lord of the Flies*. A few folk are now spinning round on the teacher's computer chair, a few bullies are pacing around at the back of the classroom, scouting out the weakest members for them to attack. One girl gets her books out to try to do some work, then, after five minutes, declares, 'I'm going to go and tell the head teacher.'

'Oh, fuck off, Claire, you grass.'

And the societal crash continues until some random supply teacher shows up because 'Mr Smith has been taken ill.' Chances are, Mr Smith got battered at the pub quiz last night, but as a kid you just accept the illness excuse because no child has ever managed to picture one of their teachers outside the classroom, never mind having fun, and God forbid drinking alcohol. I've seen Mr Smith several times now down my local, doing the quiz. It never stops being weird. There is this bizarre opinion we all have that our teachers are Mr/Mrs Sensibles that have never had a fun day in their lives, and this carries on well into adulthood. Many of you will have experienced that really creepy moment when you finally get old enough to go to clubs and you see an old school teacher in there. In a club, drinking a WKD Blue, like it's the most normal thing in the world. It isn't, mate. What the fuck are you doing here? You teach maths. You can't have fun and like maths, it's just not right. It's only upon confronting aforementioned teacher cum party animal that the reality of teachers being normal functioning human beings with proper wants and needs becomes reality.

'Hey there, Sir.'

'We're not in school now, Iain – call me Steve.'

Fuck this – I'm outta here! I don't like knowing the fact that my teacher has a first name. Some things are just better left unknown, for example what they actually put in a McDonald's Quarter Pounder or how my parents went about conceiving me. As far as I'm concerned my parents have had sex twice in their entire life – once for me and once for my sister, and the whole ordeal was quick and uneventful.

THINGS YOU LEARN AT SCHOOL STAY WITH YOU FOR LIFE – EXCEPT MATHS

Again at this point I feel the need to reiterate that this is not an attack on those in the teaching profession. You are wonderful people, with excellent first names. The point here is to show the impact school has on our formative years: our views, opinions, friendships – and for the vast majority of us these are very hard to shift or adjust later in life. The bands you like, the teams you support, the social circles you keep – it all starts at school. School is where you properly form your psyche, and should we learn any bad habits, chances are they will stay with us for a long time. So if during our formative years schools were making fundamental mistakes, this will have a huge impact long into our adult years. 'What are these mistakes, Iain?' I hear you cry. Well, let's find out, shall we?

We millennials were the first generation of pupils who could make their voices heard: we had rights and needs that school had to cater for. I'm sure everyone reading this has had a parent regale them with stories of how scary and intimidating school was for them. Public humiliation through being made to do maths in front of the class. Being forced to do PE in their pants because they forgot their kit. Or the cane. That bloody cane.

Old people love talking about the cane. It still blows my tiny little overprotected mind that it was a thing. Not only was it a thing, but it was fairly recently too – 1987 to be exact, thank you, Google. The year maternity leave was brought in for Edinburgh Council employees, thank you, Mum. That's the same year Alex Ferguson became manager at Manchester United (Mum 1–2 Google). So while Alex Ferguson was well on his way to becoming one of the most successful football managers that ever lived, a fully grown adult could (legally!) beat a child with a stick at school. At a time when you could pop into the record shop and buy a copy of Madonna's 'Papa Don't Preach,' you could also pop into the adjacent store and purchase a product that was purely for beating the shit out of children. This means that in the 1980s there were people going into the factory where they worked to spend their days making sticks that would later be used by an adult to strike a child that they weren't even related to.

However, as the legend that is Sir Alex went from strength to strength and Madonna's music career exploded, the cane died a very sudden and painful death. I can definitely see why the older generation occasionally lament its demise. I look back at my time in high school and think of all the characters that could have done with a good old caning. Would Peter Davidson have flushed my shiny Charizard down the toilet had he known that a slim rod of wood would be heading his way as a direct result?

Not that such things would have affected me. I was a surprisingly well-behaved child in my school years, and I do often wonder why that was the case. Out of school I was troublesome, a pain in the arse if you will. I was thrown out of Cub

74

Scouts for being, well, how do I word this, an obnoxious little dick. A tennis teacher once said to me, after a particularly difficult hour-long lesson during which I thought it was hilarious to keep asking, 'Miss, can I please have one of your balls?' (come on, that is *hilarious* when you're 13): 'Iain, you are the worst boy I've ever taught, and I taught Adam who stole my car.'

If that's not a quality bit of criticism then I don't know what the hell is. I think I would rather have taken the cane. But weirdly, in school I was a right goody two shoes: top of my class, head boy. I once wrote a letter to the head teacher about a boy who was being particularly disruptive, telling her that he was ruining classes 'at an incredibly significant stage of our development as humans'. I was 14 – what a prick. This is the same kid that only a year before was finding the word 'balls' hilarious.

The lad in question found out that I had written the letter and rammed a pencil through my hand. I still have a scar. Whenever people ask me how I got it I always tell them I got stabbed – I never mention which implement was involved. It does undermine the anecdote slightly if you say it was an HB. It's actually one of the benefits of being on the receiving end of a stabbing – when you tell the tale people very rarely pull you up on the details. It's essentially free rein to tell a story that makes you look like the most heroic person that ever lived. 'There were 10 guys,' 'I was in the middle of saving this dying kitten,' '... and then Barack Obama walked in and gave me a high-five!' No matter how farcical you make the story, no matter what unbelievable facts you drop into your anecdote, nobody with any moral fibre is willing to be the dick that pulled someone up on their story about getting stabbed.

Now, I don't want anyone panicking. Yes, I got bullied a bit at school, but it's fine. If you yourself are currently on the receiving end of a bit of the old bullying then fear not. It gets better, I promise. Like I've said before, I don't necessarily buy into the whole 'they're only bullying you because they're jealous' lie said by overprotective, clearly biased parents. But I can tell you this: they're doing it because they're scared that one day it'll be them being punched, or shouted at, or having troll Twitter accounts set up with the sole purpose of belittling them. They're not doing it out of hate, but out of fear. That may not help now, but in the future I promise it'll all make sense. As you get older, social media can become a good sanctuary for those of us who experienced the hell of bullying. Because you can track them down and see what has become of their pathetic little lives.

Unfortunately for me I was once picked on by a lad who is now in a very cool indie band. I'm not going to name him here, not because I feel a duty to protect his identity but because we are now fairly friendly and he's a proper lovely bloke. But the problem with being bullied by a now-successful artist who writes poignant and moving acoustic folk pop is that whereas most people go on Facebook to see that their bully has put on tons of weight and now lives in a house with their three kids they had before the age of 21, I go on to see a man with a beard

76

and guitar singing moving songs about his emotions. Being bullied is hard enough but it becomes even more galling when you realise you were belittled by the Scottish Bon Iver. That's the ultimate kick in the proverbial teeth.

I don't think bullying is necessarily a completely bad thing. Bullying hardens you up, teaches you about the harsh realities of life. Not everyone is going to like you all the time and there are some fucking horrible people out there who are going to let you know about it. Also, if we are being brutally honest, everyone reading this has at some point in their life been out in a restaurant and sat next to some little shit who clearly hasn't been bullied nearly enough. I think bullying makes you a stronger and more interesting person. Think of all the people who have achieved greatness in their life. They must have gone through real hardship to get to where they are today. I mean, Mark Zuckerberg was so desperate for friends he invented Facebook – that's a man who's been stuffed in a locker on more than one occasion! Richard Branson was so terrible with women he named an entire empire after it! In fact, whereas most people believe bullies will achieve less in their professional lives due to their lack of academic achievement, I think bullies tend to be less successful after school for the simple reason that they weren't bullied. Take away that constant threat, that drive to succeed and prove the prick wrong, and you're left with just another bloke in town on a Saturday night in his matching shirt, howling at the moon. Apart from the ones that go on to be successful, award-winning musicians and good friends. But then again he did have to move school after getting his head kicked in, so my theory still stands.

TEACHING TO FAIL

As much as the nurturing and learning aspects of school are important, I also think the real lows and hardships are just as vital in creating a balanced, functioning human being. As with modern-day parenting, schools' mollycoddling of their pupils is failing to ready them for life in the real world. School has had to keep up with the treatment their pupils receive at home. The cane now resides in the seedy world of sex clubs, where bored businessmen relive their school years by being mercilessly whipped by some latex-clad German mistress, while she tells the rich but ultimately unfulfilled banker (be careful with your pronunciation of that word) that he's been a naughty little boy.

Schools have followed the path set by our overprotective parents and tried to shield their pupils from failure at every opportunity, moving away from punishment and over to reward. So instead of the sex-pest stick, schools are now filled with gold stars, certificates and sports-day medals. Medals just for taking part. Have you ever sat down and properly thought about that? When I was at school everyone got a medal on sports day regardless of effort or ability. Although the sentiment is undoubtedly well meaning, it's basically saying: Just show up, mate, you're bound to get something. Research has shown that it devalues the awards received by those who have actually won legitimately, as well as making those who receive awards for coming last feel stupid and embarrassed, as they feel they don't deserve it. Every sports day becomes a mini-Champions League final, and every child taking part becomes a tiny John Terry getting into their full kit, including shin pads, having sat in the stands in a suit the entire game following suspension. That's what schools are doing to your children, turning them into mini-John Terrys, and no one wants that – not even John Terry.

You get awards for literally anything these days. We now give out awards to the 'most improved'. I'm sure everyone remembers the most-improved kid at their school.

'Well done, Craig – you used to be shite at javelin, now you're terrible at javelin. Here's an award!'

Craig would then appear from behind a hedge or emerge out of a bin to drag himself up to the stage, a javelin hanging out the side of his head, thinking he would be taking part in the next Olympics: 'Woo-hoo! I'm amazing at javelin. Has anyone got a pair of pliers? I feel dizzy.'

Name an award and a school will have it. There is even an award for attendance. Children are now given awards just for showing up: 'Congratulations, Timmy, your parents carried out their legal duty and managed to make you attend school. Here's a certificate!'

There is nothing wrong with boosting little Craig's confidence, even if he does have the ability to turn a javelin into a weapon of mass-destruction, but there has to be balance. Through parenting and schooling, millennials have been taught that regardless of the effort they put in and irrespective of their actual ability, they will always get something from life. This can't be healthy, as we all trundle into adult life thinking the world owes us something. The harsh reality is that when you get into the world of work you don't get rewarded for the times you do show up, you get sacked for the times you don't. And believe me, I know. I got sacked from three different jobs at university for lateness. I was furious I didn't receive *any* praise for the 80 per cent of times I actually showed up. Ungrateful pricks. Eighty per cent attendance is not a sackable offence – I should have got a bronze certificate! Besides, it used to be 72 per cent attendance, so I am in fact 'most improved'. 'Oh, what do you want, Iain? A medal?' Yes, mate, that's exactly what I want. I want a fucking medal.

You could see this as a very negative way to view life. Surely if everyone was just brought up with love and praise then the whole world would be like that? Why does everything have to be tough? And that is a lovely way to live your life. I wish we lived in a world of social harmony where atrocities weren't committed on a daily basis, where war was never even an option and Liverpool won the league every year. But unfortunately people will continue to act in self-interest, countries will still resort to warfare in order to settle disputes, and Liverpool will always struggle to compete with the finances of the Manchester Citys and Chelseas, so sadly reality will have to set in at some point. Kids have to be made aware of the fact that the world is a harsh place, because if the're not then they're in for a rude awakening. And that's coming from a man who has never managed to successfully get a proper job, never mind keep one.

CHAPTER 3

LIFE ON THE SMALL SCREEN

The Years BW (Before Wi-fi)

I have used the internet nearly my entire life. Admittedly in my younger years the internet involved an elaborate dial-up process whereby the cumbersome family computer had to be plugged in and fired up, and the initial connection involved the desktop making noises akin to some sort of robotic ejaculation. The sexy screams of the dial-up seemed to suggest that once connection had been made, the computer, overcome with ecstasy, was going to shoot a load of binary ones and zeros out of its CD drive all over its own keyboard, and then totter off to the bathroom for a little clean-up and to contemplate its own existence. Social media has also been with me the majority of my life. Initially giving out love on Bebo, or chatting to fellow Panic! at the Disco fans in Canada over online forums about our favourite tracks, I then graduated to looking in awe at how many friends Tom from Myspace had while attempting to understand why he never changed his profile picture and what exactly was written on that white-board behind his head.

All this online fun would come to a depressing and very sudden end when I heard Mum scream up the stairs, 'Iain, get off the bloody computer, I need to phone Janice!' Bloody hell, Janice, I was about to go flirt with Stacey on MSN Messenger. I mean, she isn't online right now, but she told me earlier that she would 'brb'. It is mad to think now that pre-smartphone, social-media websites only gave you a limited window of time through which to access them. Several obstacles had to be overcome before the dream of digital communication could take place. You would first have to get access to a computer, a computer that also had wi-fi access, and most importantly Mum had to have already spoken to Janice. I come out in cold sweats thinking about it now, only being able to go on social media when you had free periods in school or university as well as access to the computer room, and if that wasn't the case you just had to wait till you got home. Imagine that now. Imagine being off Twitter for more than 30 minutes. What would I do if I got to the pub before all my friends and needed to look like I was busy? I'm not a pleb sitting in a public house on my own, I'm on my phone. I could be sending work emails or managing my online investment portfolio. I mean, I'm not, I'm looking at funny memes of kittens – but the barman doesn't know that. The pleb. So although my initial interactions with social media were very different to the worlds of Instagram and Twitter, it was still there. All the information and all the friends you could ever need at the tips of your fingers. But not until, and I can't make this point clear enough, not until *after* Mother had spoken to Janice. Fucking Janice.

A WORLD WITHOUT MOBILE PHONES

There is a lot about the pre-social-media world I miss. Not necessarily because it was particularly good, I'm just nostalgic for the 'rites of passage' element of it. Gone are the days of ringing your friend's landline and having to ask their parents if Jonny's in. I use to hate ringing Jonny. The myriad of factors that had to be taken into account before the call took place. Will they be in? Is it too late at night? Will they be having their tea? A dinnertime interruption was easily your worst-case scenario. Calling up Jonny only to have his dad answer and let you know that he would call you after he had finished eating. I knew it would be him picking up, as there had been too many rings. I can't believe I didn't hang up sooner. Six rings – what was I thinking? Once it had gone past five it was game over. You always knew what excessive ringing meant: their dad at the table asking, 'Who calls at dinner time?' Or the international dad favourite: 'I'm having that fucking thing taken off the wall.'

Although his tone wasn't necessarily angry, Jonny's dad, like many dads, had this incredible skill of making even the most mundane sentence somewhat aggressive. The infamous passive–aggressive 'dad comment' has been throwing fear into the hearts of children up and down these lands since before records began. Throw into the mix that this was Scotland and it only adds to the extremity of this fear: not just an angry dad, but an angry Scottish dad. Possibly drunk and most certainly irked by something that had happened or failed to happen that day. For those unfamiliar with the accent I'm depicting here, I do not mean one of those adorable Scottish accents you get in the films. Mr Tumnus didn't pick up the phone and inform me that Jonny would meet me round the back of the wardrobe as soon as he'd finished his chili con carne. I'm talking a proper Scottish accent. The sort they wouldn't allow in a PG movie. Although I must admit if Maggie Smith had decided to do Professor McGonagall in the sort of Scottish accent I heard growing up it would have been a very different film. Maggie Smith is a brilliant actor and made McGonagall middle class for good reason. The middle-class Scottish accent has an almost sing-song quality to it, somewhat magical if you will. Perfectly in keeping with the tone of Potter and all his pals. Had she been a working-class lady from Glasgow I'm not sure she could have given those pupils the nurturing environment they required:

HARRY POTTER

Professor McGonagall, who's that behind the door?

Professor McGonagall puts down her Tunnock's teacake and approaches the door. It slowly creaks open.

PROF MCGONAGALL

Oh! It's that fucking arsehole who must not be named.

END SCENE: END OF WHOLE FRANCHISE, BECAUSE LORD VOLDEMORT HAS RELINQUISHED THE DARK ARTS AFTER SHITTING HIMSELF.

Now, I'm not saying Jonny's dad was the sort of man to call the Dark Lord a 'fucking arsehole'. All I'm saying is dads do tend to have this amazing ability to lace sentences with barbs of terror to keep those around them in check. Nothing overtly aggressive, but just enough passive–aggressive undertone to remind you that despite wearing the comfy slippers his wife bought him last Christmas, a polo shirt and some boot-cut jeans, he is still very much the alpha of the pack. And another badly timed call to the landline could very well result in him dismembering me in front of his family so that they can enjoy next week's Sunday roast in peace and quiet. Hey, I might even be used as stock for the gravy.

OTHER PEOPLE'S HOUSES SMELL FUNNY

Worse than calling the phone was going round to someone's house. Younger readers probably can't even fathom the anxiety surrounding this mammoth event – plucking up the courage to walk up to your mate's door and knock on it, not knowing the horrors that lay inside. Some families had a dog, others a scary older sibling, or worse still the overly friendly mum who would invite you in. 'Iain's here, Jonny, hurry up.' Yeah, Jonny, hurry up. I've not a clue what to talk to yer maw about, she's making me sit on your sofa and I cannot work out for the life of me why your house smells so weird. Why did other people's houses smell so weird? I always thought that growing up. It was never a bad smell, either. Not a dirty smell, just, well, not quite right. I always think of my mates' weird-smelling childhood homes when walking the dog. The minute she approaches a wall, has a little sniff, cocks the leg and then lays her scent, I get it – that wall must've smelt like someone else's house. The weird thing is that no matter what happened, my house never smelt of anything. So how come everyone else's smelt so bloody bizarre?

'Mum made spaghetti Bolognese last night for tea!'

'I know, mate, your house absolutely reeks of it.'

I would love to tell you here why this is, but I'm afraid the case of the friend's odd-smelling house remains another one of those unanswered mysteries of the world, along with why Maltesers taste better when they come in Celebrations tins and how Piers Morgan still finds work. People often say they would love to know what others think of them; I would settle for knowing what they think my own house smelt like. It's so frustrating that when it comes to smell you can never identify your own brand – because of overexposure my nostrils have become desensitised to it. It's weird that it doesn't happen with anything else. If I ate loads of custard creams, I wouldn't stop being able to taste custard creams. I would just get diabetes.

'I'M TWO MINS AWAY ...'

Whereas old-school face-to-face interaction did come with plenty of logistical drawbacks, there are a huge amount of social benefits that are now lacking as a result of social media. Punctuality, for example, is out the window. Gone are the days of meeting up at a set time at a set place then heading off for an evening's festivities. Now every social encounter suffers from a constant barrage of texts and WhatsApps of a very simi-lar ilk: 'just getting in a cab', 'traffic's a nightmare', 'missed my bus but getting on the next one', 'be there in 5', which as we all know is text language for 'I'll be there in half an hour – if you're lucky'. The luxury of being late has set the modern night out back by about an hour. No need to be on time anymore because you can let everyone know exactly where you are, all the time. And if you don't think they believe your 'sorry, I'm delayed' excuse, then simply stick up an Insta story of the traffic you're currently in. Sorted.

I remember the olden days when you would arrange to meet your mates at a pub/park (drinking establishment dependent on age), on a certain day, at a certain time, in a certain place, and you'd wait ... and wait ... and if no one else showed up you'd just go home. Like full-on, night-over, home. You might give your tardy pals a ring on the landline once you got home, but it was probably a little late by then and you didn't want to risk angering their dad. By the way, it turned out my mates were just in the pub one street down. A WhatsApp pin drop would have been really handy.

I can totally see the allure of avoiding face-to-face interaction. I can regularly be found staring at Facebook, absorbing pictures of my friends and their loved ones, while my own loved ones sit across the table from me. I mean, who can blame us? When you're out you want to spend your time with the most fun people available to you. So sorry, Mum, I know you want to talk about Karen from the office, but I've got an iPhone X with a tennis game. A fucking tennis game, Mum. This phone is so much more fun than you. Once you can return a serve smashed at your digital face at over 120 mph then we'll talk.

Actual real-life conversation, or social-media unplugged – as no one calls it – comes with an abundance of opportunities for awkward moments. Human error can lead to moments that do make you wish you were sitting behind a screen and could just turn off the horrible scenes unfolding before your very eyes and go to bed, rather than being stuck in that horrible unfolding reality. It's another factor that drives us towards social media. You can leave whenever you like, people that don't hold the same opinion as you can simply be 'blocked' and the whole time you're on it there is the opportunity, should you wish to take it, to have a cheeky little look at some beautiful (and in many cases scantily clad) lads and lasses. With social media at your fingertips adult life can just seem like a total drag, and something that is all too easy to get wrong. I guess what I'm saying in a slightly creepy way is, 'No, Sophie, I don't want to meet up for coffee. I'll just stay in the safe little world of my bedroom and scroll through your holiday photos.'

THE AUSTRALIAN HOTEL FUCK-UP (PART I)

In 2017 I was lucky enough to be asked to perform comedy in Melbourne, Australia. I know! Little old me, off to Oz to stick another shrimp on the barbie, or pay £20 for a packet of cigarettes if accuracy rather than stereotype is your bag.

I was away in France when I got the call – well, email actually, as we've already discussed how folk now tend to avoid intrusive communication that might involve any form of actual human interaction. The email was asking if I was interested in performing at the Melbourne International Comedy Festival. I remember thinking how weird that request was given that the festival had started two days before, and for the festival to be booking next year's line-up so far in advance seemed incredibly premature – not that I was complaining. There had been a pull-out days into the month-long festival and they needed a replacement. Luckily for me I was performing in New Zealand the following month, which would save the Aussies a load of money getting me home. So there you have it. I wasn't their first choice and the main reason I was on their radar was because I was cost-effective, but whatever, I was going to Australia and I was PUMPED!

The only issue was that it was very last-minute. Flying 24 hours to the other side of the world can be quite stressful and often takes a fair bit of planning. I had eight hours. Yup, eight hours. I returned from France, got to my flat and had eight hours to get my shit together. As far as mobile phone technology has come in the last 30 years, there ain't no app for that. Five loads of washing later, all of which made its way into my suitcase damp due to an uncomfortable mixture of 'lack of time' and 'my flat is in London so I don't have a dryer or a back garden', I was ready to go Down Under. There was general life admin that needed doing too. I don't know if you've cancelled a month's worth of work in one hour, but it can get quite depressing after the third or fourth call, not to mention the guilt involved in calling your parents from the departure lounge to tell them you're off to the other side of the world for a month. It ended up becoming a 40-minute conversation about what Janice had been up to that week. In hindsight I should have sent an email.

On arrival in Oz I had to check into my hotel. I was jet lagged and, if truth be told, a little hungover. I mean, a long-haul flight to me is essentially 20 hours in a floating free bar. I don't understand why every flight to Australia doesn't end like a scene out of *Trainspotting*: people falling out of the plane like they would a club at 3 a.m. on a Saturday; strangers kissing, a women sat on the stairs to the runway crying uncontrollably and shouting something incoherent about 'Kevin', and one dude who's absolutely gutted at having just dropped his kebab and chips. It's the perfect night out – or day out, depending on take-off time. Airports are the only place where time of day is not a factor in your drinking choice. Coffees at 11 p.m. or vodka at 10 a.m., it doesn't matter in the airport – there are no rules. I think 'airplane mode' is not to stop the phone interfering with the plane's technology, but rather to stop you getting hammered and texting an ex.

A lot of people still don't take full advantage of the long-haul flight. They just sit there sipping tea. Guys, what the hell are you all doing? We have just been offered free booze ... in the sky ... SKY BOOZE! Why are you idiots watching *Despicable Me 2*? Let's get on it!

Why you wouldn't need a drink after getting through the stress that is airport security is beyond me. You're brutally herded into lines of strangers and then barked at by security guards who seem no more qualified for their job than anyone else waiting in line. 'Place your liquids in this bag,' 'Put your shoes in this box,' 'IS THAT BOTTLE OVER 100 ML?'

Sometimes I wish an airline would just start up a new service that required absolutely no security measures whatsoever. Are

You Feeling Lucky, Punk? Airlines. I'd fly with those guys. None of the nonsense rules you get nowadays. It would be a utopia: people strolling up and down the isles eating food they made at home while drinking a two-litre bottle of Fanta they bought in Asda for half the price the airports charge, the whole time safe in the knowledge that, should it be required, they're able to take a shit during take-off. If air masks came down from the ceiling parents would have the luxury of putting their child's mask on first. Tray tables would never have to be stowed away, blinds could be closed during landing and people just inflate their life jackets whenever they damn well liked. Instead of the 'brace' position during a crash, you could just do a dab while posting the whole thing online because fuck you, airplane mode. I mean, yes, you might end up sitting next to some maniac with an explosive device, but if that were to happen you could just light a cigarette, take another gulp of your two-litre bottle of Fanta and enjoy the ride.

I then had to negotiate Australia's border control, primarily their unhealthy obsession with fruit. Honestly, they are bananas about bananas. (Oh, fuck you, that's a classic pun.) I think it would be harder to get a kilo of mangos Down Under than a gram of heroin. These guys really need to sort their priorities out.

'What is this white powder? Is it sugar? ARE YOU MAKING JAM?'

'Nah, this is cocaine.'

'Oh, well, in that case – welcome to Australia. Well done bringing your own. It's very expensive here.'

Luckily for me the whole fruit issue didn't really cause me much hassle as I simply informed them that I'm Scottish, and as a result was the only other person in that airport, other than the Ozzies, to harbour a genuine disgust for the stuff. Seriously, I think the Bible would have been a lot shorter if Eve had been Scottish. The Bible wouldn't have even ended up being a book. It would have been a pamphlet, a pleasant short story – a novella, if you will.

It would just be Adam approaching Eve: 'Eve, please don't say you ate the forbidden fruit and banished us from this paradise.'

'Fuck that. I ate the snake. Deep-fried that lying bastard.'

Airport security negotiated with relative ease, I jumped in a taxi, which took me into the centre of town. As I carried my heavy bags towards the entrance of my hotel, it began to dawn on me exactly why people don't drink themselves senseless on long-haul flights. The aftermath is unbearable. Being hungover and heavily jet lagged is like being hungover and heavily jet lagged – seriously, I cannot think of a simile that more appropriately sums up how awful I felt. So, just to reiterate, I was hungover and jet lagged. Worse, I was checking into this hotel late at night. For some bizarre reason there is no one angrier in the world than a night porter at a hotel. They tend to act like they don't work there or even like you're not a paying customer. It's more like you're some random drunk who's just stumbled into their front room and said, 'Hi there, do you mind if I take a shit in your kettle?'

I was once in a hotel in Leeds and when I got to my room – late at night – I noticed there were no pillows in my room. Like, none. I don't know if you've ever seen a bed with no pillows on it, but there is something incredibly depressing, almost poetic about it. I can imagine it in a modern-art gallery, or as a really good title for some singer-songwriter's debut album, *A Bed with No Pillows*.

Anyway, after checking every nook and cranny of the Leeds hotel room – seriously I checked *everywhere*; at one point I checked inside the kettle – I had to admit defeat and made my way down to reception. Now, there seems to be this belief that British people love to complain. I very much do not fall into that camp. If I'm in a cinema and someone behind me starts talking, rather than ask them to stop I just say to myself, 'Well, I'm going to say nothing then think about this moment every day until I die.' Some prick could chop my left arm off and I'd reply, 'Oh, don't be silly. It's probably nothing. I hated playing the guitar anyway.' Admittedly not the greatest approach to life, but it's got me this far so I'm sticking to it. This absolute abomination of a situation, however, could not be ignored – man needs his pillows. So to the desk I went.

'Em, hi there. I've just been to my room, and maybe this is me being a silly billy, but there appear to be no pillows ... In my room,' I mumbled, like I was playing every awkward white guy Hugh Grant has played since 1993.

The guy on the front desk just stared at me for about 15 seconds and then, without changing the expression on his face in any way whatsoever, his jaw slack as he munched on some gum, he just looked at me and with no sense of irony asked, 'What? Do you want me to go and get you a pillow?'

'Emm … Let me think … YES! I'd like you to get me a pillow, mate. Because I don't know if you've noticed, but I'm not a monk. I haven't given up comfort for Lent. I wasn't kept hostage for five years and now I have to sleep in the foetal position in the kitchen. I want a pillow. A hotel pillow. You know the type – one's not enough, two's too many. It's a fun game!'

Obviously I didn't say that. That's what I wanted to say, but as I didn't want a pube in my hotel breakfast I just said, 'Yes, please.'

WE NEED SOME NEW FONTS!

Now don't you worry, I'm not a total drip. I did let that indifferent hotelier know of my indignation through the subtle use of expression and tone. Basically my 'Yes, please' was loaded with that wonderful British tradition, sarcasm. He knew I'd used it, I knew he knew, and eventually pillows were sourced. It was the perfect conclusion to what had been a real ordeal for all involved. Although this may seem like a rather trivial example, it is this feedback that is so essential to our development as social beings.

Without feedback from others it becomes increasingly difficult to know how our words and actions are viewed by society. We rely on feedback to ensure that what we say doesn't carry with it a negative result to those around us. Social media doesn't always give you that feedback. I could stick up a photo on Instagram of me doing something abhorrent, like killing an animal, robbing a bank or voting Conservative, and the only feedback I would receive is how many people 'liked' it. Now this may be less than my usual average, but ultimately there is nothing there to suggest that my actions should perhaps be reconsidered. And yes, there is a comments section, but we all know that the comments section of anything online is populated by insane recluses who have nothing better to do with their day than roam the internet looking for things to not like. Go on YouTube and have a look at the comments section of any viral video on there and just see how many comments it takes before the whole thing is hijacked by a bunch of people who end up in a heated discussion about something often controversial and always completely unrelated to the video in question. I was on a video the other day and the thirteenth comment was: 'FUCK YOU HITLER.'

The video was Busted doing an acoustic version of their song 'Thunderbirds Are Go'. Christ, the internet can be an aggressive place. By the way, I have no idea how I ended up on that video. I think I clicked through from something cool ... it was an acoustic version of 'Year 3000'.

Research has shown that we are less likely to take in criticism or opposing opinions if they are received via a screen rather than in person. Things like body language can control the tone of what is being said, which is why the written form tends to make negative feedback feel more aggressive or combative. What we need to deal with the toxic world of digital arguments is some new fonts. These fonts could really help clear up some of the more nuanced aspects of internet communication. In fact, I'm amazed it hasn't happened sooner! It's mad to think I can instantaneously ping a message to someone over in India at the click of a button, but have no way of alerting that person to the tone in which I'm conveying it. Fancy new fonts could sort that right out. A font that suggests things like 'Although I disagree with your points, I am willing to have a calm and collected conversation about them' would, if nothing else, save me having to write that entire sentence out before every single Twitter engagement.

Yes, we have emojis, but I find them so bizarre. They're not representative of the sort of faces you make in real-life conversation. That little yellow guy with the gritted teeth – who is using that? When in your entire life have you heard someone go, 'I'm so sorry to hear that your aunt passed away,' and then start gurning uncontrollably? When have you ever said something a little bit sexy to your partner and then covered your eyes and turned into a monkey? Gone to the fridge and got out an aubergine? Emojis are just another way to separate us from our true emotions, from truly connecting to each other face to face. They're just digital hieroglyphics, showing that in some ways we've gone backwards in terms of communication. We've become like pharaohs with access to the iCloud. Instead of being buried in a tomb with all our jewels and riches, we'll just be put to rest with a phone in our hands containing all our Facebook memories.

The internet just isn't great when it comes to voicing opinion. Social media is programmed to keep like-minded individuals together, which creates what author Margaret Heffernan calls 'wilful blindness' when it comes to considering other opinions, or indeed facts, due to 'friendly alibis'.

Basically, and this is pretty common-sense stuff, we only take in opinions that match our own, as those are the ones that make us feel good. Should someone say anything that questions our beliefs we can simply filter them out. Although this may be tricky to do with someone sitting across from you at the dinner table, move that option online and it's a piece of cake. One click of the 'block' button and we're back to being right again. This internet business is an absolute doddle! You don't know who these people are, what they look like or what their background is; all you know is that they don't agree with you, which makes them wrong. So see ya later, pal, I'm off to be 'right' somewhere else!

The sense of belonging is vital to the success of social media. The more our thoughts, opinions, photos – anything, for that matter – are met with a positive response, the more time we will spend on it. This isn't just me saying this – people at the top have started to admit it. In an interview with *The Times*, tech entrepreneur Sean Parker, one of the pioneers of Facebook (Justin Timberlake for *The Social Network* fans), admitted that the site was designed to keep people hooked in a 'social-validation feedback loop' that consumes 'as much of your time and conscious energy as possible'. This is the exact same method used by gambling companies to keep their customers at the tables. And this technology is available to children, devices that are designed to be addictive, that lead to a release of dopamine, the same chemical we produce when drinking alcohol or smoking cigarettes. Yet while those products have age restrictions and tax hikes, mobile phones and by definition social media are handed out to children with no real regulation in place.

Millennials and now future generations are given access to a highly addictive product from a young age. Fifteen-year-olds in that tricky, hormone-ridden stage of development are essentially given access to their parents' drinks cabinet, only instead of schnapps it's Snapchat that they're using to numb their crippling teenage angst. This leaves the door to addiction wide open. It's generally accepted that 90 per cent of all alcoholics had alcohol introduced into their lives as teenagers; early access to dopamine-producing products leads to an increased chance of addiction in later life. Now every kid in the Western world is at risk due to the abundance of mobile phones and social media.

If you don't believe me take this little test yourself: when you wake up in the morning is the first thing you do to check your phone? When you're out with friends do you have moments when you can't help but look at your phone? Having not checked your phone in a while, do you occasionally imagine that it's vibrated in your pocket when it hasn't? If you answered yes to any of these that's addiction and addictions need to be treated. Maybe we should set up Social Media Anonymous (SMA) to help fellow sufferers. It would be so cheap. You wouldn't even need to hire a town hall – just set up a WhatsApp group.

I spoke to vlogger Caspar Lee about his mobile-phone addiction. I normally introduce the people I interview, but this kid has got 7.5 million subscribers, so chances are you know the dude already.

Interview with Caspar Lee –
'I'm addicted to my job, which is online'

> **IAIN STIRLING**
> I genuinely believe that everyone is addicted to their phone. If you wake up in the morning … I remember when I was quitting smoking and one of the tests of –

> **CASPAR LEE**
> Have you quit?

> **IAIN STIRLING**
> Yeah. I vape.

> **CASPAR LEE**
> Okay, so we'll find out what that means in a few years when they do some tests on it.

LIFE ON THE SMALL SCREEN

IAIN STIRLING

Oh, I know. It'll probably be just as bad for you. But in the meantime I vape.

CASPAR LEE

Baby steps.

IAIN STIRLING

The test of addiction is whether it's the first thing you think about when you wake up in the morning. Do you have a compulsion to do it? And I'm like, that's describing me checking Instagram, Twitter, Facebook in the morning.

CASPAR LEE

I'm reading this book called *Happy* by Derren Brown. It's really good, and it was just one of the things he said: when you wake up just don't wake up to your phone. And I've tried to do it now, and I'll just kind of lie there for, like, 15 minutes and just kind of visualise things that happened, maybe yesterday, and I'll think about the day ahead, because as soon as you pick up your phone you're probably going on Instagram and seeing how amazing everyone's lives are. And you're still in this weird dizzy state.

IAIN STIRLING

And also you end up … now that I follow so
many people on Instagram I click on the
Instagram stories and I'm there 40 minutes
for everyone's stories.

CASPAR LEE

It's unproductive.

IAIN STIRLING

So unproductive. But do you think you're
addicted to your phone?

CASPAR LEE

Yeah, so I have to consciously make an
effort not to use it. But at the same time
I think an element of my addiction comes
from the fact that I can work from my phone.
So I'd say part of it is I'm addicted to my
job, er, which is online, social media.

IAIN STIRLING

Do you not think that's what an addict would
say?

CASPAR LEE

That is actually very true. You sound like
my therapist.

IAIN STIRLING

Could you go on a laptop? I remember Simon
Sinek used to say – and I think I'm going
to start trying to do this – you shouldn't
have your phone in your bedroom, full stop.
Charge your phone downstairs. People go, 'My
phone's my alarm clock.' Well, buy an alarm
clock. They're five bucks.

CASPAR LEE

Exactly.

IAIN STIRLING

I'll buy you an alarm clock.

CASPAR LEE

Shall we do that?

IAIN STIRLING

Shall we both do that?

CASPAR LEE

Yeah, let's try it, okay. But you have to
be honest.

IAIN STIRLING

I will be honest.

CASPAR LEE

We shook hands, we shook hands.

IAIN STIRLING

I will be honest. I'll be a vapeless, phoneless guy.

CASPAR LEE

I'll start now. We're going to be amazing people.

THE ECHO CHAMBER

So there you have it. We now spend, on average, two hours of our day getting all our news and opinions from a source designed to mirror back our own thoughts and opinions, while other opposing opinions and ideals can simply be ignored and written off as 'wrong' thanks to confirmation bias from our peers. All this is deliberately put in place by the social-media companies in order to keep us happy and on that particular site – keep that dopamine coming, man, I feel so alive!

It's why people who politically lean to the right talk about social media being a 'liberal echo chamber'. As much as I hate to admit a Tory is right, in this instance they are. They're absolutely spot on. You know the phrase – even a posh broken clock is right two times a day. We are in an echo chamber and that's because Facebook, Twitter and all the rest want us to be. I'm sure there is a right-wing version too, but they can afford better soundproofing in their chamber, which significantly reduces any ungodly echo, and the whole thing is British made – obviously. The thing is, when you find yourself in a world where everyone agrees and gets along, why would you leave?

In an interview with Prince Harry on BBC radio in 2017 Barack Obama talked about this exact problem – and listen carefully, this isn't some random bloke off the street talking, this is the coolest ever President of the United States of America and he agrees with me! Fuck you, echo chamber, I'm backing my opinions up with the best thing to happen to America since Disneyland! – saying, 'The danger of the internet is people can have totally different realities; they can be just cocooned in information that reinforces their current biases.'

See, I'm right! Thank you, Mr President. From my experience in the outside world it's tricky enough to get hold of a pillow, so the allure of a place where you can have all your thoughts and opinions validated as well as stare longingly at edited pictures of all your favourite celebrities ... it's easy to see why so many of us are drawn to it. Next time your partner or parent berates you for spending too much time on your phone, just tell them: 'It understands me ... Or at least it has algorithms in place to make me feel like I'm right! Also, this tennis game, have you played the tennis game? I fucking love the tennis game!'

THE AUSTRALIAN HOTEL FUCK-UP (PART II)

I headed to the reception of the hotel, bleary eyed and heavy headed, to check into my room. I couldn't wait to be in that room. They'd have pillows, I was certain of it! I got to the desk and looked at the lady on the other side; unsurprisingly she had the sort of glum expression on her face that suggested she either a) had very recently lost a relative, or b) was working the night shift in a hotel. Unfortunately for me, fortunately for her, it was the latter.

'I'd like to check in, please,' I said.

The lady looked up at me, almost startled, like she couldn't believe I was interrupting her busy social schedule.

'Name?' she glumly replied, slack jawed and chewing gum. I think it must be a night-porter thing ...

I gave my name and she started looking it up on the computer. Although you could tell her heart wasn't really in it. She might as well have just stroked the screen and said, 'Computer says no,' like David Walliams's character in *Little Britain*, only with a little less get up and go.

'I'm afraid we don't have your booking on the system,' she grunted.

'Oh, but you do. This was booked in weeks ago.'

She didn't need to know that a mere 36 hours earlier I was in France with no plans to visit Australia any time in the near future. I couldn't have a fruitless journey to that check-in desk, even if Australians would bloody love that! I needed that bed so very, very badly. In my blind panic I started over-explaining my own name to the uninterested women: 'My name is Iain, with two 'I's. You must have it in the system.'

'Oh, we do have an Iain, actually,' she said, showing no remorse for the mistake she had made moments earlier, and her chewing gum toppled out of her mouth and on to her keyboard. She picked it up, placed it back in her mouth and kept chewing as if nothing had happened. It was so disgusting I was almost impressed. It was like watching an *I'm a Celebrity … Get Me Out of Here!* bushtucker trial live.

She gave me the room key and I headed up the stairs towards – you guessed it – my room. I'm sure there were fire exits somewhere, there was car parking for customers and that breakfast was at some point in the morning, not that she had bothered to tell me. All that didn't matter, though. I could sort that all out later. Right now it was time for sleep. Sweet, blissful sleep.

I entered my room and scoped the place out. After a quick assessment of the stuff I could nick on check-out, I looked at the bed. Things started strong: four pillows. 'Oh, Ambassador, you spoil us,' I thought to myself. I then noticed something that slightly scuppered my plan to immediately pass out in a blissful, hungover daze. On the bed lay a laptop; someone must have left it behind after they checked out. I'm always doing that. Every time I leave a hotel room I have to scope the place out three or four times, and even then I always manage to leave a charger. Some poor sod had left his computer and now it was my duty to rectify the situation.

Before returning the laptop downstairs to our cheery friend in reception, I decided to go to the toilet. Partly because I needed to go to the toilet, but mainly because I didn't want to have to confront that lady again. Not because of her dour demeanour, or for fear of where she might pick up chewing gum from next, but mainly because when I had checked in I'd had to do the one thing every man fears when he checks into a hotel late at night – ask for the wi-fi password. Never before in my life had I wished so hard for the warm, friendly confines of the social-media world, as in reality I had just asked a lady for a wi-fi password in a hotel after midnight. I might as well have bounced up to her with my pants round my ankles screaming, 'CAN I HAVE ACCESS TO ALL THE PORNOGRA-PHY, PLEASE?'

Now I had to march back downstairs, minutes after getting what I asked for, half-undressed and holding a laptop. She might call the cops! Regardless of these legitimate fears the laptop had to be returned, so I picked it up and made my way to the bathroom. As I entered the bathroom there was all the normal stuff you'd expect to see: fancy soaps, fluffy towels, you know the ones – the ones that go straight into your suitcase upon leaving. I nick everything from hotels nowadays. I don't even cover it up. Honestly, what are they going to do? I walk out the front door wearing the dressing gown like some sort of regal robe, I've got slippers on my hands like a pair of cool gloves and I even leave with the free sanitary towel on my head like some sort of whacky hat – although it doesn't cover my entire head, what it lacks in coverage it makes up for in absorbency. There was all that lovely stuff, as well as a businessman on the toilet. Just taking a shit. I've always wondered why they called it 'taking a shit'. Surely you're leaving one? I mean, I've been proud of shits in the past, but never, after a particularly good one, have I looked into the bowl and thought to myself, 'I'm having that.' You could argue that at this immediate point in my life, linguistic abnormalities could be seen as almost by the by, owing to the fact that there was a businessman defecating two feet from me. But I stand by it. 'Taking a shit' – how odd.

Now, normally when I tell this story to friends or the police a few questions rightfully arise. Firstly, how did I know he was a businessman? Simple, he was wearing a suit. Not a great look for being walked in on in a toilet situation. Suit jacket and no trousers is quite a menacing look. Upstairs it looks like you're ready for an important meeting, downstairs it looks like you are ready to jump out at someone in a park. There is nothing more confusing to look at in the world than a man in a suit taking a shit. The juxtaposition between the assertive authority of the suit and the vulnerability of the exposed legs, with the once-powerful suit trousers now sadly dropped around the ankles of a defecating human, is too much for anyone to fully comprehend. Due to the overwhelming visual information being thrown into my face, rather than apologising or leaving I just stared at the man, like right at him. He rightfully, so some might say, started screaming.

'Get out!' he shouted. If he'd had chewing gum in, it wouldn't have fallen out so much as shot across the room.

It took me a few moments to react, mainly because at first I wasn't sure if he was talking to me or giving one final big push. Maybe he was going to scream, 'Get out!' then stare down into the bowl and think to himself, 'I'm having that.' After a few moments, however, I realised he was talking to me and not his jobby. It then dawned on me that I needed to respond, but what to say? I had to be aware of the awkward situation but not make too much of a scene. I had to be authoritative but non-threatening, like the suit trousers that now lay on the bathroom floor. I knew of the delicate framework I had to operate within. Not to worry, I'm a comedian; I do talking for a living. A shitting man? I've dealt with much worse. At a recent gig in Hereford (shout out to the Hereford massive) a girl vomited mid-laugh, which brought with it mixed emotions. Sure, the place now stank of half-digested curry and two (minimum) bottles of wine, but she was laughing!

There was no way I was going to mess this up. My confidence was absolutely unfounded because what I said next will haunt me for ever, and to this day I still have no idea why I said it. It may have been because of the shock, it may have been due to the intensity of the situation or it may have been the smell coming from the fancy soaps, but I just looked a man I had never met who happened to be doing a number two and said to him ...

'My name's Iain.'

What even is that? I've not met many men who just so happen to have their dick out, but I'm pretty sure you're not meant to just tell them your name. That should have happened several hours earlier on the date. Then, as if the situation couldn't get any weirder, he fired back with, 'My name's Iain too.'

I have no idea how he thought that would help the situation. Like he thought the only reason the situation was horribly embarrassing for everyone involved was because we weren't on a first-name basis. Like there was a chance it would be totally cool that I was watching a man take a dump so long as when he'd finished we could add each other on Facebook.

The awkward silence continued for what felt – and by this point smelt – like 10 minutes, until I made my next move, and if you thought my first move was a shocker, well, wait till you get a load of this. No more words were uttered – we'd royally fucked that right up between us – so I just leaned in – that's right, I leaned in – right into his face, and gave him his laptop. We exchanged confused glances for a few more moments until I slowly backed out of the room, mouthing the word 'sorry' every step of the way.

By now I was inconceivably tired, deservedly hungover and absolutely furious. I made my way back to the front desk, where the receptionist was, and I'm not making this up, cutting her own toenails. That is not an activity acceptable in the work-place; it's not even an activity acceptable in your own lounge. In the bathroom, directly into the bin, please. I gave her a wave, she put her slips back on and shovelled a load of toenail shav-ings into a nearby paper cup, and we braced ourselves for my rant. Oh, and boy, was it a good one. I went totally tonto! I berated her lack of interest on my arrival, angrily explained the man in the suit taking a shit – at one point I think I threw up in my own mouth (but that was probably due to the booze) – there was even an unintelligible utterance about hotel pillows and then, as the *pièce de résistance*, I whipped out a printed version of my hotel reservation. Just as a quick declaration of character, I'd like to make it clear that someone else had booked the hotel for me and sent me the printed reservation. Never in my life have I ever been organised enough to print something off. I don't think I've ever even owned a printer.

The lady took it all in, looked down at the reservation, looked back up at my sweaty, jet-lagged, still-a-bit-drunk face and told me, in the coldest tone I have ever heard a human being convey information to another human being, that I, Iain Stirling, had got the right hotel room, but was in the wrong hotel. In the centre of Melbourne there is a hotel called the Adina and a hotel called the Adara, and in my opinion they are far too close together. I'll not tell you which one I ended up in to preserve them some dignity, but I left one that night, never to return again. I did, however, manage to snag a towel.

CYBERBULLYING

Despite the obvious disaster the evening in that hotel was, there are a few elements that saved it from being a total wipe-out. Although that man was clearly shocked by my entering the bathroom, he would have fairly quickly been able to tell I meant no harm. My obvious shock at his presence would have quickly alerted him to the fact that there had clearly been an administrative error. He would have felt very differently had I entered with a menacing smile and pointed at the bowl screaming, 'Are you having that?'

The way we communicate with others has so many more elements to it than just words. These social tells and signs are learnt throughout childhood and adolescence, before becoming incredibly useful tools in adult life. The knowing look, the subtle licking of the lips, when your partner says, 'I'm fine,' but it's obvious they're about to punch you. Social media makes communication easier on the whole but has no way of translating the huge amount of unspoken language there is between humans, and this could be another major problem with its ever-increasing popularity. Growing up around limited face-to-face interaction could – and in the case of millennials might very well have already – result in an inability to learn empathy.

Previously, when you insulted someone, you had to look them in the eye. You could see the anguish and upset in their face. This would, unless of course you're an actual mental, result in you feeling bad. It didn't feel nice making someone sad, so you would refrain from doing it in the future. Trial and error is how young people develop. You're nasty when you're younger because you're trying it out, and although it may be enjoyable or cathartic, the negative repercussions teach you that it isn't the right thing to do. Unless of course you're a little prick. Or Gavin from my primary school. If you're reading this,

Gavin, I forgive you. Only joking – go fuck yourself. Facebook tells me you're fat now – good.

Thanks to WhatsApp, Facebook, Twitter and countless other platforms, you can now slag people off digitally. This is known as cyberbullying or, as I prefer to call it, name-calling for lazy pricks. The problem with cyberbullying is that it allows people to do the name-calling and insulting without seeing the direct consequences of their actions. Instead of a young person being confronted with an upset face and feeling bad about causing that reaction, now we have someone looking back at a screen with a load of hilarious (if somewhat nasty) comments they made, watching the likes come rushing in with no negative repercussions for their aberrant actions. This leaves young people sitting smugly in their computer chairs thinking to themselves, 'This insult game feels good!'

Trolling is the name of the game. It's so commonplace now that we have a special word set aside for it. Christ, that's depressing. Trolling is something many who find themselves in the limelight and on social media have to deal with on a daily basis. I spoke to *Love Island*'s Alex Bowen and Olivia Buckland about how they personally handle the trolls.

Interview with Alex Bowen and Olivia Buckland –
'It's never going to go away'

> **IAIN**
> What is it, do you think, that makes people
> go, 'Ah, you're shit, fuck you'?

> **ALEX**
> I think it's just a bit of jealousy.

> **OLIVIA**
> Unhappiness.

> **IAIN**
> Do you reckon?

> **OLIVIA**
> Yeah.

> **ALEX**
> People think we've never done anything
> before *Love Island*. No one knows what we've
> done. Like, I was scaffolding in the rain,
> snow – everything. I grafted …

IAIN

I know, so the other thing – you were doing
modelling …

ALEX

Yeah.

IAIN

… working towards that end.

ALEX

Yeah, yeah.

IAIN

Do you know what I mean? I do bigger tours
now, but if you'd come to see me in
Leicester Square, like two years before
Hammersmith Apollo, and it was, like, what,
150, 200 people?

OLIVIA

People look at you and think you've just
immediately got there. You've just got to the
Apollo within, you know, six months – they've
not seen the graft you've done behind that.

I think that's what you're saying, like,
you did graft, you're a scaffolder, you had
no money …

ALEX

Yeah, people say, 'Get a proper job,' and
I'm like, 'Well, I'm doing quite well, I'm
happy, so do what you've got to do.'

OLIVIA

I think it comes from happiness, boredom and
the fact that we've allowed people to troll
for the last however many years. It's just
an acceptance thing.

ALEX

It's never going to go away, so you've
just got to accept it and be like,
'Whatever.'

SOCIAL MEDIA 'UNPLUGGED'

To become properly functioning adult members of society we
need to focus on our real-life relationships – our social media
unplugged, as still nobody calls them. So often I've been out
with friends, regaling them with one of my killer anecdotes,
and watched them get their phones out, mid-story, and just
flick through it. Mindlessly scrawling down their Twitter
mentions that they've already read a hundred times that day.
I was only halfway, you ungrateful oaf. I've not even got to the

bit about the shitting businessman yet! Talk to me, we could have a conversation. I'll give you an @ – unplugged, of course.

It took me so long to see it myself but using your phone when you're around actual people just looks rude. Period. Even having a phone visible is sending a message to everyone else that they are not the most important thing in your world right now. And no, it doesn't matter that you put it on the table screen-down. It's still there and it's still rude, and that dull grunt it makes when it starts vibrating is horrific. It's the same sound you hear when your aunty accidentally leaves her vibrator in her handbag – I'm guessing.

If we can learn to put down the phones perhaps we can restore the art of reading people's emotions, the art of empathy. The art of having a full-blown argument face to face in Prezzo. Even if it's just when you're out with your friends or loved ones. And don't take your mobile to bed with you. 'But it's my alarm clock.' Well, buy an alarm clock – or, fuck it, steal one from a hotel.

CHAPTER 4

U OK HUN?

The Power of Love ... Island

It's a shame that my first break-up took place so early in my life, as now, having somewhat unwittingly become the 'voice of love', you could say I'm something of a relationship expert. A guru. Think Casanova meets Gandhi – but mainly Gandhi. If Gandhi had sprung into the public consciousness by watching a hairdresser from Romford give some Welsh bird an infinity bracelet. And wasn't great in the mornings. Oh, and once told an eight-year-old to go fuck himself. But apart from that, basically Gandhi.

If there is one thing that voicing *Love Island* has taught me – and believe me, it's taught me *a lot* – it's that there is nothing more captivating than relationships. People often ask why the show is so enthralling, why it has captured the nation's imagination more than any other reality show of late, and the simple answer is this: other people's relationships are fun to watch.

All the will they, won't theys, the cute moments of doubt, those little glances, the first tentative approaches, then that adorable point at which true love begins. There is something mesmerising about watching two people fall in love. Like a car crash, but with more French kissing. It's instinctual; there is something programmed deep in our DNA that means we are drawn to the idea of love, of partnership – or, to use the *Love Island* vernacular, 'coupling up.'

The upside to being a passive voyeur to the whole *Love Island* experience, as opposed to one of those brave (and rather buff) souls that take part, is getting to watch all the fall-out and break-ups, the whole time thinking to yourself, 'Thank fuck that ain't me.' I don't think there is anything in this world more comforting than watching a couple have a total barney while you are not involved in it whatsoever. It feels great. Sometimes I'll hang around city centres on a Saturday just to seek them out.

I recently watched a video on Twitter, one of those random posts that show up after you get a good two hours into your brain-dead, aimless scrolling. You run out of inspirational university graduation speeches, and even the internet itself realises it has nothing left that is of any actual use or relevance to you. It was at such a point that this rather bizarre video emerged, of a New York couple having a proper full-blown domestic in the middle of the street. Clearly surrounded by millennials, who instead of offering any real help to resolve the situation simply whipped out their iPhones (other smart-phones are available) and started filming the whole thing.

Horrible that, if you really think about it, rather than seeing humans we just see content.

The argument itself was of little relevance, and carried on down the normal lines of any couple's argument, involving all the stock phrases: 'You don't listen,' 'I liked her photo, that's it, I meant nothing by it,' 'Well, your mother isn't much better,' etc. At one point, however, the man, who to all intents and purposes looked like a normal, upstanding member of the public – well, he did have a bum bag on, but then again he was American so I can only assume that sort of behaviour is entirely acceptable over there – abruptly stopped his protestations, turned his back to his partner and ran, face-first and full-force, right into a massive display window outside one of the high-street shops. It was like he was a bull and one of the shop mannequins was waving a huge red rag, rather than holding an overpriced designer handbag. On striking the window he fell to the ground, got back to his feet and just kept on repeating over and over, 'I just want you to listen.'

However, rather than releasing a little titter, perhaps having a giggle – maybe I should have popped the link into a few WhatsApp groups with the message 'Here, Craig (insert friend's name as applicable), didn't realise you and the missus had gone on your holidays. PS Nice bum bag' – all I did was think to myself, 'Yeah, I get that.' People have committed murder in the name of love, written music, made art, cut off ears and, in the case of *Love Island*, cared for a tiny little plastic toy baby called Cash Hughes. A lot of people attack religion for its divisive and destructive ways, but love, more than

123

anything else on this entire little planet we call Earth, can drive people to do insane things, both bad and good, things that they never thought possible. So that's why when I watched a man launch himself head-first into a display window outside Macy's, on a Saturday afternoon in front of a crowd of strangers who were all filming the entire event, and lie in the street, screaming into the sky, with crimson blood slowly cascading down his temple, I could understand where he was coming from. We've all been in that relationship, we've all been that enraged, that hurt, that confused, so desperate that we're capable of behaviour you would never deem reasonable in any other situation.

Although it was many years ago now, I still remember my first ever major break-up. The first one is always the worst. People say you never forget your first love, but I'd say you never forget your first heartbreak. The love now is a distant memory, but the break, which happened just a week before Christmas, is still so very vivid. In terms of how I ended up in that first proper relationship, I'm still a bit hazy on all the details, if the truth be told. It's mad to think that so many significant moments slip your memory, because as a kid you're taught through films and books that you'll never forget the special moment you first come into contact with 'the one', that person who will play such a significant role in your life for years to come. I wish there was a way to know when significant moments were approaching so you could ready yourself for the mental documentation to take place. Rather than, years later, having to delve deep into your subconscious or your

Facebook memories, depending on how snap-happy you were that evening.

From my not-so-extensive research I have managed to glean the following facts: it was some wrap party and I was very drunk and persistent, which I think we can all agree is the sexiest of all the combinations. All girls will tell you that they want a man who has a lot to say and very little ability to say it. Drunken slurs are most definitely the way to go! I would love to go into more detail, but one of the main rules of writing is to 'write about what you know', and I have no idea what actually happened. All I know is that I woke up the next day, in a bus depot in Willesden Green, with a horrible hangover, someone's phone number in my pocket and an angry bus driver screaming something at me about wanting to finish his shift. He was pretty persistent himself, now I come to think of it.

Break-ups can be tough, and the first one is brutal. That first time you go crawling back to your folks – the man that had moved out all those years ago, back on the floor of his parents' kitchen blubbing away like someone who's just watched *Marley & Me* for the first time. And I don't want to spoil the film for you, but the sequel is just called *Me*. As a man I also feel like it's that little bit harder to properly open up about your emotions. That archetype of the strong, silent type still hangs heavy over our heads. To talk about your feelings shows weakness, and who would want to be weak? Fuck being weak. Let's just bottle up all those emotions and die 10 years earlier than we probably should, thanks to some sort of heart condition, like a big, strong, silent man would do. We millennials are told we are the soft generation – 'snowflakes' is the term currently bombarded around – but for a lot of men the arche-type of the alpha male still hangs heavy over our heads, our big, strong heads that aren't even crying; it was raining outside, so fuck you!

I remember telling my dad about the break-up when it happened. Now, my dad is one of the most loving and support-ive men I know, but suffers on occasion – as I'm sure we all do from time to time – from an inability to deal with emotional moments. I know it's not from a place of ambivalence or indif-ference, but rather blind fear. You can see it in his eyes; when you try to open up to my dad emotionally he will look at you slightly aghast, like how a dog looks when it sees another dog on the telly. The initial panic will then be followed by a sentence that will demonstrate a desire to help while also steering the conversation away from any sort of emotional support towards something far more practical. The sort of sentence that tells me that he may not be able to help with that broken heart, but do I want a shelf putting up? Or to give you a real-life example:

'I love you, Dad.'

'Are you OK for money?'

So as you can imagine, with a tight, week-long schedule before old Father Christmas came flying down the chimney, I didn't really have much time or indeed ability to sort out the many emotions flooding through my system post-break-up. In fact, I had a real concern that come Christmas Eve, as Santa went to place our presents under the tree, I would burst into the living room, flooded with tears, Adele blasting out of my iPhone, and just start dry-humping the leg of our friend's soft, red satin suit and scream, 'This year for Christmas I just want to be held!'

Unfortunately for me, and an entire film crew, this turnaround was tighter than first expected. Because the next day, the very next day, I was filming a TV show. A presenter-led children's TV show. And the presenters in question went by the name of Jedward.

THE JEDWARD FUCK-UP (PART I)

Now, before we jump head-first into this, I would like to make a few disclaimers. First, this event was several years ago, and since then I have gone on to meet Jedward several times in numerous different situations, and the nation's favourite twins (ignore those lassies off *Fun House*) have always been nothing other than delightful and accommodating. The way I will proceed to describe them in the following story is no reflection on them, and is very much tainted by the incredibly difficult situation I found myself in during filming. And second, I have slightly exaggerated their personalities in order to increase the enjoyment of the read. Or have I? No, seriously, I have … a bit. At any rate, lads, if you are reading this – if in fact you can read – I just want you to know you are lovely boys, a credit to Ireland, and I look forward to seeing you again soon.

With all that said and done, there is a very good question you have every right to ask regarding the predicament I found myself in, and I'm guessing it goes something like this: 'How did you, Iain Stirling, find yourself agreeing to film a children's TV show with the much-loved boy band/twins/faces of Shake n' Vac Jedward?'

Well, truth be told, this story took place around the same time that I told that eight-year-old to go fuck himself. And, as we have already ascertained at the beginning of this book, I wasn't in the best place emotionally. I had just left CBBC full-time and was still getting a foothold in the stand-up world, so I had time in abundance and bills to pay. My agent (at the time) had also told me the fee, which was very acceptable, especially given that it was for a mere day's work. I'd be in, do my job and be out before you could say, 'My name's John and my name's Edward, and together we are Jedward.' And actually, I had a weird existing relationship with the lads due to my time as a CBBC presenter. As they had a massive younger following they were in the CBBC office (our studio) on an almost weekly basis, so I'd met them before and, like I've already said and would like to make very clear, they were lovely lads.

They tended to get more airtime than most other stars when I was at CBBC owing to the fact that Hacker T. Dog and I had a running joke where we would call them Jed and Edward. Not a particularly hilarious gag, and certainly not one you would keep running for three years of live television; however, every time we said it on air the emails and our Twitter feeds would fill up with angsty tweens, Jedward fanatics who would angrily remind us that his name was actually John not Jed, and some of the more full-on fans would threaten us with illness and death and other disproportionate punishments that seemed totally unnecessary given the nature of our crimes. Ah, the internet, how I love you. So the joke kept on running for no other reason than pissing off trolls is fun.

So with all that in mind, particularly the money, I'm going to be very honest with you here and say it was a lovely bit of money – don't get me wrong, not thousands, but for a man who at the time had no girlfriend nor regular income, a few hours in the presence of the 2009 *X Factor*'s sixth-placed entry seemed rather alluring. I mean, what a series that year's *X Factor* was! I'm sure we all remember that fateful Saturday night when our boys Jedward eliminated Lucie Jones in the sing-off. We all remember the amazing scenes when Simon Cowell picked the lads, having chastised them the entire series. It was a real turning point in *X Factor* history, actually, and cited by many academics as the turning point in its move from a singing competition into flat-out Saturday-night entertain-ment show. Oh boy, Saturday nights were alive in 2009! My parents used to watch it from behind a massive desk while giving out their own critiques between acts. My dad would even wear his trousers offensively high. You could see his testi-cles. I didn't like it.

I got on the train to Bath, where the filming was set to take place. I remember even before I set off being slightly pleased by the time of that train. Normally with location filming you have to arrive farcically early, before the general public get there, in order to make the whole process a lot smoother. The last thing you want when you're running around the mean streets of Bath with Jedward is normal people just kicking about in the back of shot shouting things like 'Jedward, I love you' and 'What you did to Lucie Jones is one of the biggest miscarriages of justice within the music industry'.

For some reason, however, the BBC had booked my London train for 10 a.m., meaning I wouldn't get into Bath until the afternoon, which famously is when Lucie Jones fans are at their most prevalent. The late start was great for me as it gave me plenty of time to carry out my favourite night-time activities over those first few post-break-up days, which as we all know are to lie awake all night, regretting every life choice you've ever made while eating ice cream. It wasn't just wall-to-wall regret, though, don't you worry about that. I'm not totally pathetic. In order to break the monotony I also had three beers and two cries. So all in all a very productive night was had by my good self. I think at one point I started writing a poem, until I realised how fucking pitiful that was, which might have been what started the initial crying. It was certainly the cause of the initial beer.

As I approached Bath I was in relatively high spirits. The day was looking like it was going to be wonderfully short, and in no time at all I would be back up the road to Scotland for Christmas, where I could feel regret, loneliness and anguish all over again, but this time in the sanctuary of my parents' house and there would be a tree, in the lounge, with lights on it! I bloody love trees. It's a real shame that we don't bring forestry into our homes at other times of the year, like an Easter oak or a Halloween eucalyptus.

I arrived at the station and met one of the production managers in the car park. She was a lovely, smiley woman, although if you looked deep into her eyes you could tell that she had spent the last three months trying to run a television production fronted by the beloved Jedward, every day making sure they were in the right place at the right time. Her eyes suggested that it was tantamount to directing smoke. Really annoying, nasally smoke. Just imagine the Chuckle Brothers, but with less common sense and more annoying catchphrases. As I entered the car she handed me a hotel key.

'Fuck me,' I thought. So glad I thought it. I had spent the last couple of days in complete isolation, so by this point thinking and talking had all but merged into one. It had started to make trips to the shops very embarrassing for everyone concerned: 'You've lost everything, you fucking useless twat ... Sorry, what's that? A bag for life? Nothing's for life!'

This 'fuck me', however, was a 'fuck me' of joy, like when your girlfriend gets dressed up for a night out and walks into the living room looking radiant or you check your bank balance and it's significantly higher than you were expecting, because not only was I getting paid good money for a short day's filming, but I even had a hotel room to get myself ready in.

Although many celebs try to make TV out to be a very glamorous lifestyle, it rarely is, and this is never more so than when children's TV budgets are taken into account. I could spend the rest of this book telling you about the times I've had to get dressed in woods or public toilets. Once, in Stratford-upon-Avon, I spent the day dressed as Shakespeare's wife (despite my best efforts, the footage is on YouTube) and it rained constantly, but as none of us had dressing rooms our only option was to wait in the public library. I sat in the non-fiction aisle dressed as a woman, dripping wet (not like that – get those minds out of the gutter), and just had to wait. The real low was when I saw a seven-year-old boy whisper something to his mum, she gave him something out of her purse and he walked over to me, damp and in drag, to hand me a single, solitary pound. It was one of the sweetest things anyone has ever done for me, and yet still one of the bleakest experiences of my life. Pity from a seven-year-old – do you know who I am, mate? I've met Jedward, you little shit! I did take the pound, though.

Today, however, was to be nothing like that. Today was going to be one of the good days, all a little bit showbiz – a few hours filming, in my own clothes and with a hotel room to get ready in. I. Could. Not. Wait. I turned to the lady driving me to the hotel and asked her how long I had to get ready.

'Oh, you've a while yet,' she said. 'We won't be eating till around seven. But don't want to be much later as we're all up so early for filming.'

My heart would have sunk had it been able to go any lower than the gutter of piss and shit that it currently resided in, where it spent its days sifting through old Facebook photos of the ex. In my hotel room I immediately called my agent. Now, at this stage in my career I wasn't massively high up her list of priorities. When I called I was amazed she answered, as our previous phone-based relationship normally involved me calling her two or three times and then her calling me back a few days later, reminding herself of my name and letting me know that the thing I was calling about wasn't happening any more or had fallen through for some unknown reason. In hindsight I'm aware that the reason was because someone more famous was free to do it.

Of course, the reason she was so keen to answer on this occasion was that she had realised the mistake she had made when offering me the gig and was waiting on my call, during which I learned that the offer wasn't in fact a great deal for a single day's filming, but rather an absolutely fine deal for the three days' filming I had unwittingly signed myself up for. The day after the first and to this day biggest break-up of my life I was to spend three days in Bath with both Jed and Edward. And, as had been the case my entire CBBC life, the days were going to be long, involve early starts, and feature Jedward and fancy dress.

During dinner I spent most of the time telling people 'I'm fine' while they continually asked why I was so quiet. I'm not a huge fan of people who do that whole 'I'm fine' thing when it is clear from their tone and manner that something is up. I just think, 'Tell us what's going on, you fucking coward.' I've driven myself insane worrying about why someone was slightly off with me when in fact their issue was completely unrelated to me. Is that because I'm a kind heart and a friendly soul or because I'm a massive egomaniac who needs every situation to be about him? I don't really care what's wrong with you, as long as I don't have to feel any guilt for it. I think I've just answered my own question. If you're not having a good time just go home. Or talk it out. It's the guessing games that always leave me in an existential crisis. In this particular situation, however, production were paying for dinner, so telling them the truth would have done very little to settle the mood: 'My agent didn't read the contract properly, my girlfriend's left me and, quite frankly, I would rather have chlamydia than spend my days in the run-up to Christmas filming some awful kids' TV show with Jedward.'

So instead I stared into my carbonara, resisted the temptation to drown myself in it and just tried to sit the whole thing out. Jedward didn't come to the dinner – I have no idea why. Apparently they were busy learning their lines, which, if the next day was anything to go by (spoiler alert), was a massive fucking lie. Over dinner we were told the premise of the show. An American girl, who was also at the dinner, and I were going to team up with Jed and Edward in a series of challenges. We would learn facts about Bath during those challenges, and at the end there was going to be a quiz, with the losers doing a forfeit, which would involve them carrying the winning team by chariot to one of Bath's famous, well, baths. There would be three locations and a costume change in each one. We could go back to the hotel for these changes, but it would be much quicker and very much appreciated if we could change in the van.

The American girl enthusiastically agreed to all of this, and I desperately attempted to match her energy levels while imagining how many strands of spaghetti it would take to create a noose strong enough to hold my weight. Once dinner was completely done and dusted we all had a beer. (Which, as a quick aside, is my absolutely least-favourite amount of beers. No beers – absolutely fine. It's your life, beer is full of calories and very often people don't want to feel groggy in the morning. Loads of beers – yes fucking please. We're all stuck in Bath with Jedward, I can't be the only one here who didn't picture their career turning out like this – let's get absolutely hammered. But one? *One*? That's what I want to feel like just before I go to bed, slightly bloated and with a crippling desire for more beers.) After the singular beer was drunk, we were informed that Jedward had requested to meet the American presenter and me before bed.

After another quick drive (one of the very few benefits of the insufferable one-beer rule – people can still drive), we headed up to Jedward's room – yes, ROOM. These two lads, now in their early twenties, still shared a twin hotel room like a modern-day Bert and Ernie, only slightly less capable of teaching toddlers how to read and count. On entering, feeling slightly bloated and in need of more beer, we met one half of Jedward, who gleefully informed us that his brother was currently in the toilet taking a dump. That's about the only thing they didn't do together, thank God.

Eventually, our star returned from dropping the brownies off at the pool, and it was definitely either Jed or Edward, I honestly can't remember which one. We had been informed over dinner how to tell them apart, but at this point the fact that one had a slight scar above his upper lip caused by a childhood accident was way down my list of priorities – behind things like 'try not to cry' and 'don't mention it's creepy that they wear matching pyjamas'. After any break-up a lot of people feel the need to boast online, let their other half know all the fun and interesting things their soul mate is getting up to now the shackles of the relationship have been shed. Presumably with the hope that one little post might make them forget all the bad stuff, instantly regret their decision and come crawling back. I drafted a post on Facebook:

'Just had one beer, my new favourite amount of beers, and now a Z-lister is taking a dump five feet from my head!'

I decided not to post the update as I felt it may not have had the desired effect, even with the *crying with laughter* emoji. It would merely have reinforced the idea that she made the correct choice.

We talked about the next day's activities. 'Getting dressed in a van – that's so cool!'

Jed or Edward screamed, clearly very spritely after his late-night stool. The American girl also screamed, matching the twin's excitement, so I just decided to agree, mustering up as much excitement as I could physically muster. That was my best option, I had come to realise. Just agree and eventually this will all go away.

After the excitement of hearing we were going to be getting changed in a small moving tin can in front of complete strangers, we looked for a few minutes through the scripts Jedward clearly hadn't read, then, after politely declining a very generous offer to jump on the beds, I returned to my room. I drank the two beers from the hotel minibar, taking me above my insufferable one-beer total for the night, and went to sleep/lay awake staring at the walls and stalking my ex's Facebook page to see if she'd become friends with any boys I didn't recognise. You know, just the standard stuff.

Just as a quick head's up for anyone that goes through a break-up in the future, check *all* your apps. You never know which ones will be there to taunt you. There were a really bad few days for me when her Uber account was still linked to my email, allowing me to spend endless hours on Google Maps working out which houses she had been to and gone from that day, driving myself to near physical and mental breakdown. But now, thanks to the break-up, I lived on my own and I could shit with the door open. So not all bad!

DIGITAL DISPLAYS OF AFFECTION

I do find it hilarious sometimes to see people post about how mad those contestants on *Love Island* are, baring their souls on a TV show, and then you click on their Facebook profile to see photos of them and their new boyfriend, a post about how much they hate their boss at work and a passive–aggressive argument with their ex in the comments section of an old photo. Whenever you talk about your relationship online you are broadcasting to an audience. It may not be as vast as that of ITV2, and it may not be accompanied by the witty commentary of a stand-up comedian and good friend of Jedward, but it's still an audience. Don't believe me? Go onto Facebook right now and change your status to 'single' and see what happens. Pandemonium will break out, folk you haven't spoken to in years will appear out of nowhere telling you how special you are and how they've always felt you deserved better. Hell, a few exes might even slide into your DMs to offer you a shoulder to cry on.

The Facebook relationship status is such a good example of how much trickier relationships have become in the online era. Everything has become so – there is no slow-building romance. Gone are the days when you would slowly start to introduce a partner to each of your groups of friends, hoping they passed the tests laid out by each, and hoping that one of your more, shall we say, loose-cannon mates didn't end up drinking too much and telling the new love of your life the story of that time you took a shit in the bush! Hypothetically speaking, obviously.

Now you just go to the settings on your Facebook page, hit 'in a relationship' and boom! All your friends know, your family know, that guy you got drunk with once in Prague knows, everyone knows. Does everyone need to know? Does my old driving instructor really need to know if I'm in a loving and stable relationship? Probably not. He just needs to know how to efficiently teach someone the safest way to perform a three-point turn. I'm always caught between this weird world of sharing my relationships online but also trying to keep things personal. I put a lot of my life online so it would then seem weird not to talk about my girlfriend at the same time, wouldn't it?

Why do we even have to consider these things? What a weird world we have created for ourselves, where not sharing personal information with the outside world seems as much of a statement as sharing it. Relationships aren't like trips to the gym or avocado on toast – they are far more precious, and sadly a lot more volatile. If you are reading this and are anything like me then you'll have the same fear I do when I post online, that one day my luck will run out and the person I'm with will realise the error of her ways and go running for the hills, leaving me looking like a total mug, with posts all over my socials telling the world how truly in love we both are. That is a hell of a lot more embarrassing than getting dumped off an island – I can tell you that for free. So maybe these islanders aren't as mental as we all first thought.

THE JEDWARD FUCK-UP (PART II)

The next morning – and boy, was it morning, 5 a.m. to be exact – the show's runner came into my room brandishing the first costume of the day. He entered in a very apologetic manner and with a very specific look in his eyes. With my years of telly experience I knew it to be a look that said, 'I'm so sorry, but I'm about to ask you to dress like a fucking moron and parade around in public.' It was like Stratford-upon-Avon all over again, only this time I had no girlfriend to ring up and have a right old laugh with about how ridiculous I looked. The first costume was of an old theatre popcorn seller, complete with a small tray of ice creams and popcorn. I had a little hat, like the ones people wear in panto when they're playing Buttons. In fact, pantomime would be a very apt way to describe the look in general.

'Where's my career?'

'It's behind you.'

'Oh, no it isn't.'

'Oh, yes it is.'

Out to the van I went to see Jedward dressed as Victorian gents dancing to some random Britney Spears tune barely audible due to the terrible speaker built into their iPhone. That's what you want first thing in the morning, to be forced into pantomime attire and be made to watch two folk you barely know dance to Britney Spears like they've just dropped a couple of pills at G-A-Y. Today was going to be a long day, and it was going to be soundtracked in its entirety by the Princess of Pop. What had I let myself in for?

We got to our first location, and although we were early, Bath is a very popular tourist destination and, as it was so close to Christmas, the schools were off and the place was absolutely hoaching with families, mainly young families, the worst type of families. New parents desperate to let their son or daughter look at anything for long enough so that they might get a second's respite from not having to be fully alert at all times. Also, don't forget that at this stage Jedward were not long out of *The X Factor*, and they ain't the most inconspicuous looking of lads. Jedward are capable of many things, but let me tell you this, 'blend in' ain't one of them. Basically they can't do that, or spell. These seem to be the big two.

So then cameras showed up at a quite middle-class tourist destination and fucking Jedward leapt out, dressed as Victorian gents. They even had the tops of their pipe hats cut off so their quiffs could pop through the top. Did I mention that? I really feel I should probably mention that. They looked like an aristocratic Scotty 2 Hotty, should you be fans of niche noughties WWE references. And just in case that wasn't enough, 'Hit Me Baby One More Time' was still blaring out their iPhone. People took notice – and photos, so many photos. The rest of us just wanted to get the filming done, but Jedward didn't care. There were people around and they wanted photos, and by Christ Jedward were going to give it to them. They couldn't sign anything, sadly. That whole spelling issue really let them down on that front.

Filming continued throughout the day but was a slow and laborious process. The boys were all over the place. At one point Jed lost his shoe; later on we found Edward up a tree, eating someone's shoe. The whole thing was a nightmare, a nightmare I faced the entire time broken-hearted and dressed like Buttons. I went on my ex's Facebook to see how she was getting on. She'd gone for a spa day with the girlies, a guy called

Darren was tagged into the post. Who was Darren? I didn't know Darren. She'd never mentioned Darren. Turned out Darren was a gay 34-year-old radio producer originally from Hull. Luckily for me, Facebook privacy settings weren't what they are today.

In an attempt to try to numb some of the pain I reached down into the bright-red tray on my waist and opened one of the tubs of ice cream – it had melted. Which was artistically appropriate given the context in which it was being eaten, but it didn't help my mood any. At this point the director ran towards me: 'You can't actually eat them, Iain. They're props. You can have one once we've finished this scene. We're just looking for John – he ran off chasing a pigeon!'

After taking in all the information that man had just given me, I shovelled the cold, melting liquid into my face using the little plastic spoon that came with the pot, a spoon that was entirely too shallow for the consistency of the ice cream. It dripped onto my hand and made it look like my finger was crying. 'Another possible Facebook post,' I thought for a split second, before changing my mind and licking myself clean like a massive, hairless, depressed cat. I must have looked like a sphinx on a comedown, who for some reason was dressed like Buttons. Although if the music in the background was anything to go by, maybe he had just got in from a night out at G-A-Y. A small child then tapped me on the shoulder. I turned, he smiled at me and I smiled back, his little face giving me some respite from all the stresses of that day. He then reached his hand out, placed it in mine and gave me a pound.

Once Jedward were finally located we managed to film our first few scenes. I would honestly love to give you a breakdown of exactly what took place that day, but most of it is a blur. One oddly vivid memory was of lunch. We got taken to this weird school hall-esque building and everyone got Marks & Spencer sandwiches, which I for one was more than happy with. Jedward, however, had recently discovered sushi. They sat at a table on their own with platters of raw fish, the whole hierarchy of the image accentuated by the fact that they were still dressed as Victorian gents – lording it over us peasants with our pathetic tuna-and-mayo sarnies.

The reason this memory is so particularly vivid is because, as well as eating their own body weight in rolled rice, the lads were constantly playing about on the phone. Let me just say that again so it sinks in: *the* phone. That's right, as well as sharing a hotel room, which is weird enough but you can just about fathom a situation in which it is acceptable – I mean, don't get me wrong, sharing a room means that shitting with the door open is out the question – Jedward also shared a phone. Just the one. That's two fully grown men, one phone. How they managed it is still beyond me. Imagine all the private information and personal conversations you have daily through your hand-held device. Was there anything these two didn't do together? Well, as I'd discovered the night before, shit, but apart from that how did they function independently of one another? I simply couldn't give up the independence my own phone affords me. And even though singledom had been thrust upon me, I was truly independent now! No one could tell me what to do. Well, apart from the director, who was about to give us our final filming script.

The finale was upon us and everyone was super-excited, and by everyone I mean Jedward. And their excitement wasn't necessarily directed towards the idea that despite everything they still had a TV show, but rather towards what was undoubtedly the moment they had been looking forward to all day. Yes, you guessed it, getting dressed in a van. We had to make our way to the final bath to do the quiz. The winners of which would also get to go in the bath. And this was all going to take place while we were dressed in togas.

So as the van made its way to the bath, I found myself sat in the back of a van with Jedward and a random American girl, all in our pants, trying to work out how to put on our togas. The entire time Jedward played the same song, on loop, from 'the phone', and that song was 'Under Pressure' by Jedward.

We got out of the van and the good news was that the place was deserted; the bad news was that this was because it was pouring with rain. Normally you hold up filming when it rains to allow it to pass or at least lessen slightly, but we had spent too long chasing Jedward around parks as they scared pigeons or lip-synced to Britney Spears, as well as waiting for them to remember all the lines in that script they 100 per cent abso-fuckinglutely hadn't read, which meant we had no time for luxuries like, oh, I don't know – not having to stand in the freezing cold rain in togas. So we did a quiz that no one really gave a fuck about apart from Jedward, who despite showing the most enthusiasm, demonstrated by far the least amount of knowledge.

I don't know if you've ever seen Jedward being quizzed on Roman history, but it is a very frustrating process, made all the more annoying for me as I was deliberately trying to lose, because believe it or not, going for a dip in the pissing-down rain in a random public bathing pool in Bath with one of the members of Jedward was not my idea of a reward. Normally when you win a pub quiz you receive something like a £50 bar tab. What you're certainly not after is some awful company and a possible verruca. So with an impressive demonstration of blind idiocy, which included me answering the question 'Where did the Romans originate?' (answer: Rome) with 'Narnia', I was off the hook.

There was, however, a slight issue I had overlooked, which was that the losing team had to deliver the winning team to their pool in the cart. So that's how I spent my final hour before my much-needed Christmas break: in a toga, in the rain, dragging a man-powered cart while one of the Jedwards screamed 'Faster' in my ear for all eight – yes, eight – takes. My agent quit comedy management a few months later. Apparently her heart wasn't really in it. I honestly had no idea!

OUT OF SIGHT, OUT OF MIND ... STILL ONLINE

On returning from my ordeal with Jedward I was ready to just get away from it all. Most of us love to constantly update people on what we are doing at all times via social media, and Jedward were no different. With all the costumes and silly locations they were in their element, constantly putting up selfies of us running around, being silly and generally having a whale of a time in Bath. My ex obviously knew I was going on that filming trip, and she undoubtedly checked out Jedward's profile a few times to see how I was getting on, having noticed my online silence. She would have seen me smiling, dressed up, narrowly losing a quiz, and she was probably slightly hurt by how well I was getting on with the whole situation.

That's the problem with our online lives. If only Jed or Edward had snapped me sipping on that lonely beer, or licking melted ice cream off my knuckles like a sad cat, then and only then would she have had the full picture. Thanks to social media, now we all have to experience the neverending break-up. It's not enough anymore to move out or stay inside; there are a number of electronic connections that need to be severed before the relationship can truly be 'out of sight, out of mind'. This isn't always as easy at it sounds. To leave someone's social-media page can often come across as a lot more aggressive than you intend. This makes sense for the social-media companies because they want as many people with as many connections as possible, so they use terms such as unfollow or unfriend. I don't want to unfriend anyone; I just don't want to have to look at their photos anymore because it makes me sad.

These loaded terms mean that many of us often stay connected with people we can't really stand. The number of people on my social-media timelines who are insufferable is insanely high, simply because I don't want them knowing that I have culled them from my online life.

Everyone has had that horrible moment at a social gathering when you spot at the other end of the room someone you have recently removed from all your social-media platforms. In real life they are pleasant enough, bordering on enjoyable company, but when they move online they become a grade-A bellend, using the internet in the most insufferable of ways: retweeting praise, humble-bragging and boasting about successes like they have some horrific egotistical monster deep inside their soul that remains dormant until it is exposed to any sort of wi-fi connection. Well, the 'horrible moment' in question will come when that person approaches you and utters the five words that can make even the coolest of cats hyperventilate with pure dread:

'Why did you unfriend me?'

Ahhhhhh, fuck. What do you say? The truth? No chance. You can't tell someone at a dinner party that you unfriended them because 'when you get behind a keyboard for some bizarre reason you become an insufferable wanker.' They're nice in real life, you're enjoying chatting to them, you don't want to make them feel bad, so instead you just have to lie. You have to act like you have absolutely no idea how Facebook even works, like you're the most electronically inept human alive, like you wouldn't know what a laptop was if one hit you in the face. Say something about how that's happened with a lot of your contacts recently, mutter something about algorithms and then just end the conversation, pretend to choke on something, leave the party and hide in the bath for a month. That's what a proper grown-up would do.

It's easier to just stay connected. This is even more the case when it comes to exes, as to leave them would seem such a statement, one that you're not quite ready to make at this early stage of the break. Yes, I'm filing for divorce and taking the dog, but let's stay friends on Facebook ... I'm not a monster. This opens us up to the most horrific of the post-break-up nightmares – and sing along if you know the words – 'accidentally stumbling across your ex flirting online'. It's an awful thing to see, the harsh reality that what you once had is over, and even though you knew they were probably flirting with other people – hell, you've probably even done a fair bit of it yourself, you dirty dog – when confronted with the reality of it, it's all too much to bear.

It can also be hurtful watching your partner being more fun and flirty with someone than they were with you. You probably spent the past few months of a relationship that was no longer working not being as playful and tactful as you once were – so seeing someone else getting that sort of attention can be double hurtful. I mean, they weren't like that with you – and you put years of hard graft in! It's like when your dog runs off to get cuddles from some random person in the street, and you just stand staring at your once loyal canine companion cuddling up to any old stranger and think to yourself, 'What about me, you ungrateful prick? I pick up your shit!'

This idea of your partner moving on quickly is compounded when you understand how we behave online when it comes to relationships. When you first meet someone you are attracted to the amount of online interaction you have is incredibly high. For many people the idea of finding love online has become totally normalised. Gone are the days of the late 90s ands early noughties when dating sites were seen as pathetic and desperate, reserved for the socially inept who on the first sight of a woman would simply ejaculate the word 'sorry' all over the walls of a restaurant and then retire to their parents' basement to continue their game of *Dungeons & Dragons*. I remember a TV sketch show in the 90s that would depict the people who submitted VHS tapes – yes, you heard correctly, TAPES – to different dating companies, in which they would state their name, age and a description of an ideal partner. In case you haven't already guessed, the depiction of these characters was less than complimentary. Cat ladies, sleazy bankers and spotty, socially awkward teenagers would all take turns trying to catch their very own George Clooney to very little avail. If you aren't familiar with what I'm talking about, a quick trip to YouTube (have you heard of it?) and a search for '*Smack the Pony*'s dating sketch' will let you know exactly what I'm talking about.

Now, however, online is the way to meet people, and in many ways it makes a lot more sense. Online you get to know someone, what they're into and get a decent idea of what they look like (at very particular and calculated camera angles and with good very lighting). To the modern dater the idea of waltzing into a bar and licking the face of a stranger you barely know can seem totally preposterous. 'You want me to kiss Karen? I don't even know how many followers she has on Insta!'

It may appear on the face of things that your ex is ploughing head-first into a brand new relationship with someone they barely know, like what you had together meant absolutely nothing and, despite the years you spent together, through the good times and bad, they're already ready to move on to pastures new. When in fact the reality is that they are simply in the early stages, still treading water and trying to get to know that person on a more personal level, and as a result have no real-life personal contact. In fact, when it comes to a relationship conducted almost entirely online, the reality is normally that, rather than meaning they are madly in love and indifferent to what the outside world makes of their clearly unbreakable love, neither party has made the incredibly brave move of asking for the phone number. Remember when the phone number was the first thing you would aim for, the Holy Grail of the night out? Back in the day of Britpop and Nokia 3310s it was the first thing you would ask your mate as you crawled, hungover, into the pub for a much-needed Sunday lunch and Bloody Mary: 'How'd it go, man? Did you get the number?'

The idea of asking someone for their personal number now seems far too intrusive. Asking someone you like for their phone number? I'm not a fucking serial killer, mate! How about I ask for something slightly less intrusive, like her bank details or a lock of hair? So instead we all go on the tiresome social-media merry dance where we follow, then friend, then like several posts, maybe even make a few comments, before working up the confidence to go 'sliding into the DMs', and then and only then is it appropriate to go asking for those oh-so-precious digits. And if you don't want to take my word for it, I've also read things written by clever people who can call upon things I believe you call, and I hope I'm saying this right, 'facts'. In a post on Facebook's data-science blog, Carlos Diuk gives us the cold hard numbers.

> During the 100 days before the relationship starts, we observe a slow but steady increase in the number of timeline posts shared between the future couple. When the relationship starts ('day 0'), posts begin to decrease. We observe a peak of 1.67 posts per day 12 days before the relationship begins, and a lowest point of 1.53 posts per day 85 days into the relationship. Presumably, couples decide to spend more time together, courtship is off, and online interactions give way to more interactions in the physical world.

'The physical world'. That's what academics are now calling it, that magical moment when two people come together and meet in person to have a chat, share ideas, shake hands, kiss cheeks, smile at one another, you know, all that stuff regular, functioning people do. It will never stop blowing my mind that this is the way we talk about human interaction these days. 'The physical world' is no longer the norm, but just another mode of communication lumped in with all the 'likes', DMs and comments of social media. No more, no less. Just another 'world'. Whereas before, people spoke about moving things 'to the bedroom', now we conduct so much of our flirtatious interactions online that a move to actually meeting someone has been pushed several rungs up the relationship ladder.

We can't be too many years away from people telling their mates about that time they were chatting online with this absolute stunner and, once the mood was just right, they then decided to take things to 'the physical world'. How would you even go about doing that? Tell a few jokes which are not only witty but also manage to remain within Twitter's very strict character limit, then once the LOLs are flowing you then send a few memes of your favourite cocktails and when the mood is just right, perfectly set, you go in for the kill: 'Hey baby, how about we take this ... to the physical world?'

The next thing you know, the passion of the moment takes over and you're carrying out all sorts of unspeakable acts: shaking hands, helping each other with your coats and then, when you feel it's all getting to be a bit too much and the physical levels are off the chart, that's when you both decide like proper consenting adults to share a starter. You absolute heathens – I hope you're using protection! So with all this flirting taking place online these days, it's easy to see how you can catch your ex's profile and imagine that they're just getting on with their new single life without a care for your past at all.

And, of course, given that people tend to big up their life over social media, with the low points conveniently filtered out, it's no surprise that the online profile of someone who has recently gone through a break-up will be a million miles away from their actual day-to-day mental state. You would really have to make some awfully awkward posts online post-break to give an accurate depiction of what single life is really like after a long-term relationship, and I don't think they are the sort of posts the rest of the world are ready to see. 'Hey guys, so I'm in the house alone, just deciding whether to have a wank or a cry #choices *laughing-face emoji*'. No one needs that.

SWIPE RIGHT

In terms of its online popularity, dating owes a lot of thanks to its good friend Tinder. You cannot escape the dating behemoth that is the swiping system! At my age there are two camps of people when it comes to the app: singletons, the majority of which have found themselves at some point or another on the app judging and swiping their lonely evenings away; and those in long-term relationships, who are absolutely devastated that they've never had the chance to experience it.

Anyone who has been single during the Tinder revolution has had their phone grabbed by a coupled-up mate who then starts frantically scrolling through, trying to relive their single life by utilising your carefully choreographed Tinder profile. And the best thing about the whole thing is that the friend in question is absolutely innocent. Tinder has become the world's greatest loophole to the rather frustrating monogamy rule folk seem to insist on these days – come on, lads, it's the twenty-first century, let's have some fun.

I used to enjoy having my happily spoken-for friends manically swipe and chat their way through my Tinder app; it was oddly life-reaffirming, like being single wasn't all that bad and there were in fact many benefits to the often lonely life. That being said, there is always that horribly creepy moment when one mate (normally married) would show just that little too much interest in the whole thing, like the use of the app was less a 'bit of fun' and more absolute escapism.

What was it that Tinder did to make online dating so acceptable that even married men can flip through their friends' iPhones without fear of repercussion? Well, first of all it eliminated the requirement for you to say you were actively looking for a partner. Dating sites of yesteryear would make you state what it was you were looking for in a partner. A bit of company? Some fun? Marriage? These tags could make someone feel like they were coming across at best a little bit sexually deviant, and at worst desperate. 'I'm looking for a husband' probably isn't the best way to kick off a first date, not when you saunter into the local Wetherspoons wearing a wedding dress, trying not to get tartar sauce on the engagement ring. Similarly, the chances of finding long-term happiness understandably drops if you broadcast over the internet that you could really do with a shag. Not that that's a bad thing. I've had shags in the past and they're wonderful things – can't recommend them enough! What Tinder did was just let you be online, not even stating your relationship status, just there to chat. It helped taking the stigma out of the whole process. I mean, who really gives a fuck about what someone is after initially? Chances are you're talking to the person's married friend anyway.

Finding love is a massive part of becoming an adult, and there is, however, a worry that Tinder is a hindrance rather than a help. Post-break-up, everyone has heard that infamous phrase 'there are plenty more fish in the sea', and continuing that analogy, if dating used to be like fishing by the side of the river, online dating is more akin to fishing on an Ibiza booze cruise in a glass-bottomed boat, and forget the rod because you've got dynamite. You're right, mate, there *are* plenty more fish in the sea; in fact, truth be told you can't bloody move for fish, or men, or women or whatever the hell you're into, mate. This is the internet, my man, knock yourself out! Next thing you'll be crawling around on that boat's glass bottom with a mermaid and a few of your fellow booze-cruise companions, having the time of your bloody life putting haddock in places you didn't even know existed! OK, sorry, the whole fish analogy just got slightly too creepy.

On top of these fantastical and endless relationship possibilities, the clever tech folk responsible for the Tinder app, as with all other online social platforms, haven't underestimated the addictive nature of our good friend dopamine. The satisfaction you get from hitting one of those heralded 'matches' on Tinder is like ecstasy for the soul. Oh my God, fish has never tasted so good. That's me done with the fish analogy – I promise. Nothing brightens up a boring family dinner more than a little bing from your pocket letting you know that Peter from Hull thinks you're really fit. Oh Peter, you cheeky little minx, let me finish this Viennetta and I'll be right with ya.

This does mean that dating can become like an addiction to novelty without substance. People start collecting matches like stickers in a sticker book, and having conversations merely to pass the day, rather than to try to nurture any sort of genuine connection. This has created a phenomenon called 'ghosting', in which you meet someone lovely, get that match, you start chatting, you have so much in common – you both love sushi and Busted (Charlie is your favourite, obviously) – and then after a week or so the replies just dry up and you're left to get back on the glass-bottomed boat and start the whole sordid process all over again. Now *that* was the last fish analogy – honestly.

Research has shown that around 80 per cent of messages on dating apps go unanswered. The idea of just cutting someone out of your life has become common practice rather than a dastardly deed. I mean, we all remember the *Sex and the City* episode (fuck off, you watched it too) in which Berger (babe!) breaks up with Carrie by leaving her a Post-It note? Well, at the time he was made out to be a complete and utter monster, but by modern-day standards the guy's a fucking gentleman!

We all seem more open to the idea of 'ghosting' one another for the simple reason that we millennials live under that constant pressure to improve. Dating apps, and Tinder in particular, have simply transferred that need into our dating lives. We are all now constantly trying to 'trade up'; we're now on a constant look-out for a better 'match'. YouTube sex and dating expert Shallon Lester, author of dating memoir *Exes and Ohs*, explains it perfectly:

> Among achievement-driven millennials, it can feel almost foolish NOT to be relentlessly searching for someone better. While baby boomers stayed with one partner, one job for their entire lives, we have swung to the opposite end of the spectrum and feel like if we aren't constantly questioning whether something (or someone) is good enough, we're somehow traitors to our generation.

Not only are we getting used to break-ups, we're getting really fucking good at them. It can't be good for settling down and getting on with our adult relationships if we are willing to move on the minute something better slides into our DMs. Given the amount of break-up practice I've had at this point in my life, if I had to do that Jedward filming today I wouldn't have a miserable experience at all. Chances are I would join the band. We'd be munching sushi and discussing album titles by lunchtime – in togas, obviously.

CHAPTER 5

THE GRASS IS
ALWAYS GREENER

We're All Fake Happy

One of my best social-media-unplugged relationships is with my good mate Steve. Steve has been there for me through thick and thin. He was the first person I turned to after I told that eight-year-old to go fuck himself. Oh, I once told an eight-year-old to go fuck himself, have I mentioned that? Because I still find myself screaming in the shower every morning over it, so I hope it left some sort of lasting impression on you. Surely I can't be the only one who does that in his morning shower? Every now and again, as I stare up to the shower head and the water batters off my face, I have a horrible flashback to some stupid thing I said or did years ago and feel the need to either shudder or scream that memory out of my head. These memories are not ordered, they don't link and they haven't come up in my conscious mind for quite some time. But there they are, served up to me by my subconscious as I wash off my Head &

Shoulders. It's like my mind realises what a warm and calming place the shower can be and needs to sully the moment with a general reminder that I'm an actual moron – miles off the proper adult I long to be!

'Hey, Iain, me again. Remember that time you kissed a girl you really fancied as part of a theatre piece you were doing at the Edinburgh Festival, and she approached you after? If I remember correctly, you were about to ask her out until it became horribly apparent that she had only come over to let you know "you're not really meant to use tongues when kissing on stage." Oh, you do remember! Good. Oh, and another thing, you once told an eight-year-old to go fuck himself.'

For the record the play in question was improvised, so I hadn't anticipated the kiss coming. I had never done theatre before so was unaware of the etiquette involved in a 'stage kiss', and I hadn't realised I'd even used tongues. Not that I'm making excuses. I mean, even typing this now ... oh God, tomorrow's shower is going to be a fucking nightmare.

Anyway, Steve and I go way back, and recently we decided to go on our first holiday. Lovely stuff. Nothing too taxing, just a few days away in Copenhagen, as our friend Tom was over in Sweden doing some amazing work with IKEA, so we thought we would give him a bit of a change of scene. So Steve and I recruited another friend, Tim, and made our way over to Denmark to meet our good old, flat-pack-loving pal Tom. What could go wrong? This was going to be a lovely getaway, not to mention a really strong week for our Instagram stories with all the shenanigans, scenery and avocado on toast we would be experiencing.

Going away can become exciting due to the much-needed shot in the arm it gives your social-media feeds. No more Boomerangs of your legs reluctantly carrying you into work of a morning, or boring gym selfies with the time clearly plastered on the bottom so everyone knows what an early go-getter you are. I mean, 'leg day, in the morning' – well, aren't you a modern-day Arnold Schwarzenegger! Holidays, much like our entire lives, are slowly becoming performance pieces, content for our adoring followers/audience to consume. The world is your stage and now, thanks to social media, everyone has an audience. As a generation we've all become performers, performing constantly for free for the entertainment of no one in particular. Just so that at the end of the day we can watch our own lives back as satisfied audience members. Surely that must be one of the tricks to happiness? To be able to do something and not require an audience. It's difficult, don't get me wrong, as social media is essentially a multibillion-pound industry's answer to our need to be accepted and validated. What else is Instagram really other than your seven-year-old self riding a bike for the first time while screaming, 'Look, Mummy – I'm doing it! I'm doing it!'

Do you know what I miss because of all this instant communication? People. Like, do you know when you've not seen someone for a bit – say they've gone on holiday for the week – and then you meet them again and you get to be all happy they're back and excited to find out what happened when they were away. Maybe you've got some juicy gossip for your best mate on their return home. At high school my mate Craig went into hospital for four days with a broken ankle, and when he got out I was the one who got to tell him about Gary fingering Kerry in the park and some teachers catching them. I know! Imagine how much fun that was for me. It would have been ruined if it were just another bit of information plastered on the Twitter wall along with football scores and what some prick with a Union Jack display pic thinks would improve Britain's immigration policy. I got to tell Craig. Me. I got to see his little face light up, I saw the Diet Coke shoot out of his nose because I timed it perfectly to coincide with him being mid-swig. We exchanged a properly human moment: physical, palpable, real. Oh Christ, I'd missed him!

Don't you find it somewhat unsettling that now, thanks to social media, when you return from your hols they don't even ask how your holiday went – they tell you: 'Spain looked amazing, mate. That church was *so* beautiful.'

What church? How did you know? Oh yeah, it was on my Instagram story, now I remember. The funny thing is, a friend's opinion of your holiday is generally speaking much better than yours, as they've seen it through the rose-tinted (or the 'Melbourne-filtered', if you prefer) lens of your social-media feed. Don't get me wrong, in many ways they are right. The church was sick. Unfortunately, I didn't post the three hours it took to find the fucking place, the stench of manure coming from the neighbouring field and the general apathy I felt around 20 minutes after entering, having lit a candle and then realised that there is very little else to do in a church if you don't have faith and have taken all the photos you'll need. There's only so many Jesuses on windows I can enjoy. Why does he love being on windows so much? Still, looked good on Insta, so every cloud ...

I HATE MY SELFIE

Thanks to social media we have become increasingly good at putting filters on things. We can snip out the bad bits, enhance the good and generally make our lives look like an absolute dream that no real-life functioning adult can live up to. This can have a big effect on our self-image. Our relationships are increasingly moving online, meaning we are failing to get a full and frank picture of how other people's lives are really going. By its very nature, online communication is very self-centred. It's estimated that during face-to-face interaction around 30 to 40 per cent of chat is about yourself; that rockets up to 80 per cent when the conversation is moved online. We now have a load more relationships that are impersonal, very egocentric and filtered to look much better than the reality would support. How many times have you put up a beautiful, filtered photo of you on some lavish night out while sitting on your couch in your pyjamas with a horrible tomato-ketchup stain dribbled down your front?

I imagine you picture me writing this very book as the incredibly handsome and charismatic funny man I've become famous for ('oddly attractive' – *Heat* magazine). The reality is that I'm unshaven and wearing the same pair of grey joggers as I have for the past three days. I'm now so dishevelled that the other day on a bus, which seems to be a popular hangout for unwashed bearded men, a mother told her kid, 'If you don't behave the scary man will come and tell you off.' I looked around, only to come to the harrowing realisation that the 'scary man' was in fact me. ME! I've got 100k-plus followers on Insta, you cheeky cow!

After engaging in these online relationships it starts to feel like our own lives aren't good enough. We don't dress as well as Claire, our job isn't as exciting as Dave's and, boy, is Karen's newborn cute. Obviously Karen doesn't put up pictures of all those shitty nappies or her face after a week of three hours' sleep a night because baby David has decided 4 a.m. is the perfect time to wake up. This filtered reality causes us to question our own lives and decisions: 'How does everyone seem to get it so right while I always seem to get things wrong? Oh Christ, I'm covered in ketchup again.'

Things become even more dire when we factor in the notion that millennials haven't built up as many real-life relationships as previous generations, so instead of turning to a person for help we turn to a device, and the whole thing starts all over again. It's a very dangerous cycle that needs to be broken. Get off those phones, go see a friend and talk, maybe even grab some lunch. You'll feel better, I promise! But maybe leave off the ketchup, yeah?

We only see what others choose for us to see, and that can make us feel like our own lives don't measure up. This can lead to an increase in mental-health issues such as depression – and believe you me, the evidence is there. More and more children are taking time off school, citing 'depression' as the reason; suicide is now the highest killer of men under 45; and other mental-health-related deaths such as drug overdoses are also on the rise. Although our relationship with mental illness is improving as a society, we still have a long way to go. Many people, particularly (but by no means exclusively) men, still struggle with the stigma attached to seeking help with mental-health issues. Even the way we talk about mental health can be a little confusing. I mean, how many times have you heard someone say, 'He *is* depressed'?

He *is* depressed? No, he *has* depression. It's an illness, not a definition of who someone is. You wouldn't do that with any other medical condition. You would never watch your dad limp into the living room and start screaming, 'I *am* gout!', making him sound like he was a bit-part character from the *Guardians of the Galaxy* franchise rather than a pensioner who just needs to lay off the cheese.

To help with your own mental health it is important every now and then to take a step away from social media. Even celebs are taking a break from the constant bleeps, rings, likes and friends, deciding to spend the time elsewhere. Ed Sheeran recently took a year off social media, and talk of social media's negative impact is increasingly making its way into main-stream media. Online life isn't real. It lacks the imperfections and nuance that make up an actual person, and to compare yourself to someone online is not a fair way to gauge your own successes and failures. But how do those who make a living portraying these so-called 'perfect lives' – AKA social influencers – feel about the effect their posts might be having on those that follow them? I spoke to Alex Bowen and Olivia Buckland about just that.

IAIN

I've got a bit about living on my own and how lonely it can be. I mean, it's not fucking dark or hard-hitting, but every time someone comments on that I think, 'Oh good, you know that.' And the same if you guys put up a picture, like 'I've got no make-up on' or 'I've got a massive spot on my chin today,' and a few girls comment and you think, 'Oh my God, I get that same thing.' Does that help you as well?

OLIVIA

Yeah, it's like normalisation, isn't it? It's making things normal that were always normal but are now considered not. You just saying you live on your own, you sometimes feel lonely – there could be someone in your audience thinking, 'Oh my God, I feel so lonely, I'm the only person in the world that feels like this …'

IAIN
Yeah.

OLIVIA
And this is such a good thing about social media and we do forget that - like, we forget how good it is sometimes. It's always the negative, like you were saying earlier.

IAIN
Exactly. So how do you go about getting that balance, because Instagram's essentially your job, do you know what I mean?

OLIVIA
Yeah, it sounds really weird, doesn't it?

IAIN
And you've got the time and energy to make it and you've got to make your job look as good as possible. But at the same time, you don't want a bunch of kids thinking, 'I need to look like that and be like that.' So how do you balance that? Have you consciously

thought, 'Right, well, I'll put this many posts that are sexy and a few that are daft,' or how do you go about it? Or is it just what feels right?

ALEX

I think you've got all your social-media posts, the paid posts and stuff like that, all your promotional work, and then people want to see you being an idiot. They've watched us on TV being idiots and that's where they loved us. So that's how you've got to be on your Instagram, taking a selfie with a dog, the dog licking my ear, running into one of theirs, getting away from it – they love that kind of stuff because they feel like they're in your life as well. Because Instagram, it's in your phone, you're connected to everyone.

IAIN

Yeah.

ALEX

That's what people want to see. So, I think that's the way it should be, 50/50.

THE GRASS IS ALWAYS GREENER

OLIVIA

And with that, I think some people here
would say that they calculate what they've
put on and what they post and how they
present themselves. But I think with us, we
don't actually do that. We are quite
ourselves.

ALEX

Plus, for example, if I put a picture on of,
a paid post, and it's with our big Canon
camera that we've got, it looks like a
proper photo-shoot picture. And then I'll
post a picture taken on my phone if I
haven't got the camera. On the camera phone
I'll get more likes than the one with the
camera, because people feel like it's just
off your phone, quick, done, connected.

OLIVIA

It's just normal.

ALEX

Whereas if it's a picture of me and her,
it'll get double the likes a solo post would
get. Cause that's what people want to see,
me and Liv together.

OLIVIA

I do think it is hard. Like, if I was smoking, I wouldn't put a picture up of me smoking, so that's where you do have to calculate sometimes what you're putting up. I mean, I don't, but I wouldn't because I know the girls - I wouldn't want to do that. But …

IAIN

Yeah, you didn't want to - you don't want a 14-year-old that thinks you're the best thing in the world …

OLIVIA

Cause I smoke.

IAIN

… going, 'Oh, that looks so cool.'

THE COPENHAGEN FUCK-UP (PART I)

In Copenhagen, Steve, Tim, Tom (who were now hilariously being referred to as Tim and Tom the Flower Pot Men) and I were smashing the social-media output. First night saw the four of us get the obligatory 'lads in matching shirts in front of a white wall' pre-night-out photo – for social-media purposes, obviously – and then we went to a ping-pong bar. No, not that sort of ping-pong bar, you dirty bastards! This was real ping-pong, but with a twist. I hope it's big all over Denmark because it's a properly awesome idea. Basically, there is one ping-pong table in the middle in the bar, everyone takes a bat and then forms a circle around the table, moving in a clockwise direction and taking a shot each time they reach the front of the queue at each end. If you miss, you're out. Last person standing at the end wins and then you all go again. When it gets down to three people you are basically sprinting around the table the whole time. It's thrilling, intense and embarrassingly beyond my fitness abilities. It's that simple and, best of all, you can't hold a bat, a beer and your phone.

Don't get me wrong, the minute I was eliminated I documented the shit out of this bizarre mainland Europe activity to show all my followers back home what an interesting and unique time I was having, but those three minutes during ping-pong bouts were social-media-less bliss. I mean, this just wouldn't work in the UK, some idiot would refuse to leave once they'd been eliminated, and you know there would be some wanker in a vest top who had brought his own bat taking the whole thing too seriously. But this was Denmark, everyone was chill and it was SO. MUCH. FUN.

After all the beers were drunk and all the ping-pong was played – by the way I was absolutely the best and didn't get knocked out early pretty much every game – we decided to move on. I don't know if it was the alcohol from the beer or the endorphins from expertly playing a sport, but as a group of four fairly straight-laced males we made a rather left-of-field decision. We were going to go on a trip to somewhere a little bit naughty!

Now, when I say sensible I mean properly sensible: Tim and Tom (the Flower Pot Men) were both teachers at some point, and Steve once went to Ibiza for a week and got through eight books. In fact, they are such a responsible group of lads that I was very early on identified as the weak link in the four and not even trusted with a key for the flat we were staying in, as 'chances are I would lose it'. Can you imagine that, me as the liability? I don't know if you are the unreliable one of your friendship group, but it really gets you down after a while. Never best man at a wedding because chances are you would mess up the stag do or lose the ring. Never trusted with any real task for fear of it going awry. Always told a time to meet 15 minutes earlier than the actual time because they have (correctly) predicted you're going to be late.

Don't get me wrong, this was amazing as a teenager, as you never had to do anything, administratively speaking, ever. You were never the one who had to book the bowling alley, check the cinema times or collect the money to pay for Laser Quest (what a way to celebrate your exams ending that was!). As adulthood dawns, however, it does start to get a bit emasculating always sitting in the back of the car on holiday because you're not trusted to be involved with the rental, or sitting at the children's table at social events 'because Craig booked it and decided on the seating plan, plus he's still properly pissed that you lost the wedding ring.'

Anyway, keygate was a long-distant memory by the time we left the ping-pong bar to hit the town.

THE LEGEND OF THE DISPOSABLE CAMERA

When I was growing up, holiday photos would be an administratively difficult, near-impossible activity. You would first have to take the photos on a non-digital camera. No preview screen to show you how the photo went. Forget about the worries of lighting, angles or even exposure – you couldn't even check if you had managed to fit yourself into it.

With old-school cameras you just took a photo and then had to wait until after the holiday for the big reveal. 'How did you get to see the photos?' I can hear the youngsters reading this book cry. Well, after your holiday, once you had safely returned home and the tan had started to fade, you would go to the pharmacy – yes, pharmacy – and *pay* to get the things printed. You would hand your film over to a random and often creepy-looking man who would go into a back room and develop them in a dark room. If you're too young to know what a 'dark room' is, they are those things you see serial killers developing pictures of their victims in during episodes of Scandinavian crime dramas. You would have to wait for hours, sometimes days, unless you were a millionaire and then you would get the hour-long service. Once the physical print-out was in your possession you would rip open the paper packaging and flick through your masterpieces: 'That's just my thumb, that one's too bright, you've left the lens cap on there, that's my thumb again.'

At the end there would always be two or three photos of the dog, your back garden or your dad randomly sitting in his living-room chair, taken by your mum, who was trying to use up the last of the roll. It was almost like a legal requirement. You can't leave unused film on a disposable camera – it's like going to an all-you-can-eat buffet and leaving before you feel so full you could actually vomit. You couldn't imagine all that rigmarole now, as cameras today are so user-friendly all you need is one simple click and you're free to post away. Hell, nowadays you're more likely to accidentally post a picture online than anything else, even if mums still have a super-human ability to mess it up completely, managing to post pictures of thumb-covered images in a Facebook album entitled 'My life'.

This explains why people idealise their lives online now. If you don't have to travel to the shops to get photos printed and wait four hours to get the things back it frees up a hell of a lot of time to filter, nip and tuck. And the ridiculousness of social media seems particularly apparent when it comes to things like holidays. As a kid you would dread going round to someone's house after they returned from holidays because you knew that at some point in the evening you would hear those dreaded words: 'Should we get the holiday snaps out?'

No, you fucking shouldn't. Twenty-five minutes of dinner plates, cathedrals and that one time Cindy got her hair braided. Every now and again the fit big sister would show up in a swimsuit, but that didn't justify the previous 20 minutes of torture! I think about those moments now when I look at Instagram. That's all it is, just a constant stream of holiday snaps, and I waste hours going through it *all*. What are we doing? What is it that we are so drawn to? Maybe we should go back to the good old days of film and Kodak disposables. I'm sure the creepy man in the pharmacy would love to have us back. I wonder what he's doing now? I mean, if you're that interested just watch an episode of *The Killing*. You'll get a rough idea.

THE COPENHAGEN FUCK-UP (PART II)

Despite our foursome having the rock 'n' roll credentials of Il Divo, we decided to take a cab to Christiania. For those not as undeniably cool as me, eight books and the Flower Pot Men, Christiania is a famous freetown in Copenhagen founded in 1971. A 'group of hippies', to quote its own website, took over an abandoned military barracks and set up their own alternative society with its own rules, independent of government. The inhabitants of Christiania want to get away from a society they feel places too many restrictions on their freedom, and tourists go there to, well, smoke weed, basically.

'Hang on a second, Iain,' I hear you cry. 'You, Steve and the Flower Pot Men (a name that had gone from odd to weirdly appropriate) are going to smoke drugs? What would your mothers say?' I know, I know. Mother Stirling would not be best pleased. I'm actually going to get a copy of this book made specially for her with this chapter taken out, so nobody tell her. Seriously, not a peep! No one likes a grass. Unless that grass is in Christiania – AM I RIGHT?

Once we got in to Christiania, which looked exactly like what you would expect an abandoned army barracks turned hippie refuge to look like, we came across our first hurdle in operation 'let's take drugs like the absolute total lads we all are', and that hurdle was, well, getting drugs. A fairly major hurdle, I think you'll agree, but not for the reason you may think. The availability of the aforementioned substance was in abundance – you literally couldn't move for the bloody stuff. Stall after stall lined the streets, each with neon lights and handmade price boards. It was like a Christmas market, but with very different trees for sale. Santa would need more than a mince pie to satisfy the munchies he would have after leaving this place!

The issue we 'total lads' had was asking for them. Firstly, Steve and the Flower Pot Men had decided they didn't want to smoke any of the weed – it seemed a little too naughty. They hadn't done it before and were worried about the potency of a joint so wanted to start things off with a nice little cookie. This would seem an easy enough request; however, Steve was, and still very much is, lactose intolerant, so not only would we have to negotiate buying the cookies, but we would also have to ask if 'the cookie had any milk in it', which I felt would really eat into the 'laddy', drug-taking personas we were trying to convey to the Christiania inhabitants.

Secondly, where I grew up drug dealers were scary people who sold illegal things, not someone you just approach on a holiday with your specific dietary requirements. It didn't feel like you could treat one of these stalls like an Apple store, asking for information, getting help on the product that was right for you. The guys weren't 'geniuses', they were drug deal-ers. Obviously the reality was that the majority of their busi-ness was selling to tourists who need information and guidance, but my stupid male ego wouldn't allow me to show any weakness, so I opted for strutting up to the stall and demanding the items I required. This meant I could leave the stall taking no hit to my fragile ego, and so what if I left with no working knowledge of what the hell I had actually bought?

We spotted a stall. I mean, I say spotted, there were hundreds of these stalls spread around the centre, but this one felt right. Steve and the Flower Pot Men held back, frozen by fear. For a bunch of men nearly in their thirties it must have looked pathetic – like a bunch of 15-year-olds hanging around outside an off licence, choosing the tallest one to go in and try to buy some cider with the £5 they've scraped together between them that day. I'm six foot two, a solid two inches longer than the other three, so I was given the job. I couldn't believe I had been trusted with an actual job. Who's the unreliable one now? It was exhilarating, but with great power comes 'great responsibility', or at least 'the job of buying cookies and a joint for a bunch of losers who never embraced the whole "weed phase" in their teens'. Up to the counter I went to ask, 'Do you sell edibles?'

To this day I have no idea where knowledge of that word came from. I must have heard it in a movie or a comedian maybe mentioned it on stage at a gig we had both performed at. It was the proper term for a 'drug cookie', but you can't say 'drug cookie' to a professional drug dealer – he would have laughed in my face! Luckily I said 'edible', and much to all our relief he did have them and handed me a box of three cookies. Originally the plan was to buy two. Two cookies, four 'absolute legends': it seemed like a perfect amount. However, as I intended to smoke that night I didn't want to take too much, so I just bought one for each of them. My logic being that it would free me from the cookie situation and I could just have the smoke – I know, what a genius. It would also mean they would have double the amount of cookie, but what's the worst that could happen? It's a cookie. No one has ever had a bad experience from a cookie. They're called cookies, for crying out loud.

I paid for the goods – I couldn't tell you how much the guy asked for them, as I was so full of fear and confusion. I just gave him a fistful of euros and ran. We also picked up a few beers and headed to a bench in the centre of Christiania. I lit my joint and the guys tucked in, very timidly, to their cookies.

The whole atmosphere was somewhat movie-like. Christiania, with its abandoned army barracks, looks like something out of *The Walking Dead* made even more peculiar with the constant but very definite waft of weed ever-present in the air. Maybe that's what *The Walking Dead* is, just a bunch of folk who have smoked way too much weed and are now wandering around with a homicidal case of the munchies. We started chatting, drinking, eating, smoking and drinking some more. Throughout the process we'd check in with Steve to make sure the cookie hadn't disagreed with his frankly below-par digestive system, but thankfully all seemed well.

About 20 minutes in I started to feel the high come. As someone who doesn't take cannabis regularly, if at all, the experience was so exciting. Like the first time you drink, or kiss a girl, or play *FIFA* Ultimate Team (I would take a game of *FIFA* over cannabis any day of the week), a bunch of emotions started flooding through my body. Dazed and confused, Tim found a bunch of seats inside a bar about 30 yards from where we were sitting. As we went inside, the drugs really started to take hold.

It's impossible to explain exactly what I was feeling, but every time we moved location I was acutely aware of my changing surroundings: air temperature, the music playing, the texture of the seats – every subtle change became so incredibly significant to me. Like each change in location was a jump cut in a movie in which I was the principal character. The whole thing became not just overwhelming, but ridiculous. I couldn't cope anymore. Why are we in this bizarre army barracks cum hippie refuge? Why have a bunch of men, long shot of their teenage 'experimental years', decided to pick now to experiment with cannabis, and more significantly, 'HOW TINY ARE THESE FOOTBALLERS' FEET? THEIR SHIRTS ARE TINY BUT STILL HAVE NUMBERS ON THE BACK!' Oh yeah, I should probably mention that by this point we were playing table football. Why? God knows, it seemed like a good idea at the time.

While the other three quietly played the game, occasionally nibbling on their lactose-free, drug-full cookies, I just burst out laughing. Not 'Oh, that's a good joke' laughing, either. I'm talking fully fledged maniac laugh – imagine *that* scene from *Ghost*, but instead of helping me with my pottery, Patrick Swayze was tickling my armpits. I was laughing like a nine-year-old watching *You've Been Framed*. My laughing continued for what felt like 30 seconds, but I've later been informed it was more like 25 minutes, and eventually a very Danish-looking barman – tall, bright blue eyes, blond hair in a slight mullet, or at least that's what I've been told he looked like, my eyes were very watery at the time – approached us and said in the most Danish accent possible (and if you don't know Danish just think really Dutch, like Mike Myers when he played *Goldmember*): 'Can you please go and be high over there?'

So off we went to be 'high' over there in the chill-out corner. I had no idea why one corner of a room was more acceptable to be high in than the other, but I was nowhere near 'with it' enough to question our Aryan friend's opinion. After a few minutes of 'being high' in my designated area, kinda like a child's soft-play area but for a bunch of adults who were all slightly giggly and all of a sudden very hungry, I decided to head off to the loo. It was on my return that the entire mood of the night changed …

Returning from the bathroom admittedly took longer than it probably should have, as I spent a good seven minutes finding the toilet door and another ten admiring the texture of some guy's coat. However, once the toilet had been done and the coat had been stroked I immediately headed for the bar. Yeah, that same barman might have still been there, but I had been in the designated 'high' area now for a good while and needed a drink – I'm sure he would understand. As I approached it became clear that I was no longer that high up on his priority list, as some guy was clutching his chest and screaming, 'I'm having a heart attack!' The barman, who had clearly been briefed at the start of his shift, started asking him to 'please be high over there', pointing at the corner of the room I had enjoyed for the past hour or so – but this guy was having none of it: 'No, mate, you don't understand – I'm having a heart attack!'

I made my way to the bar, partly because I really wanted a beer, but mainly because I wanted to see what this mad man would come up with next. When I got there I realised that the madman was Tom of the Flower Pot Men, and he was not in a good way. I peeled him, still clutching his chest, off the bar man and apologised profusely. Tom told us that he was having a bad trip (shock) and that some sugar might help level him out. We picked up a packet of Haribo (Tangfastic) from the bar and walked Tom to the benches outside.

'I'm sorry, lads. I'm so sorry,' Tom kept repeating, and decided to continue repeating for a solid 30 minutes after we had accepted his apology. I don't know how many apologies need to be accepted for a cannabis-based outburst, but according to Tom it's roughly 279. While Tom sat munching on Haribo and apologising to everyone who passed, including the guy with the awesome coat, I had a read over the cookie packaging to pass the time. I read the back, then read it again, and then once more just to make sure I hadn't made some silly mistake in my drug-fuelled glaze: 'This cookie contains the same amount of cannabis as approximately five to six spliffs.'

Five to six! Tom, Tim and Steve had each eaten an entire cookie having never had any weed in their lives previously. I told the boys and there was a palpable mood change. Now Steve and Tim weren't just looking at Tom; they were looking at their future. Tom had gone from someone who's 'had a bit too much' to a human tarot card, and the guys didn't like what they saw. They knew they had taken the exact same amount and were moments away from phantom heart attacks and aggressive apologies. They pre-emptively started to guzzle Haribo (Tangfastic) like the kid with ADHD at a six-year-old's birthday party.

We quickly made our way to a taxi rank to get home before total pandemonium set in, ducking between army buildings, hippies playing folky guitar music and all the stalls that had got us into this mess in the first place ... but it was too late. Steve and Tim had joined Tom on the wonderful trip down trippy cookie lane. Outside, no taxi would take us, mainly because the three lads were screaming things like 'Why is the street so loud?', 'Is that a dragon in the back of your car?' and everyone's favourite, 'Seriously, man, I'm having a heart attack.'

So we went down that classic millennial route and decided to book a cab online. The cabbie wouldn't know the state we were in, and thanks to him having all the information on his phone we wouldn't give the game away by chatting either. So long as Tom could stop screaming 'I'm having a heart attack' for five minutes we'd be home. The taxi arrived, we all got in and the man started to drive. Never has a cab drive been more quiet in my entire life. For some unknown reason we had left Tom in the front, and after 15 minutes or so of unbearable, eerie silence, he attempted to ask the driver a question. Unfortunately the driver didn't understand Tom's question as his English wasn't great. I am, of course, talking about Tom's English: he could barely speak and asked the driver: 'So what are you now? Cos I was but wasn't sure if it still is.'

To this day no one has any real clue what Tom wanted to ask. There was something beautifully philosophical about it, and at least it killed some more time before we got dropped off. A drop-off that was taking a lot longer than any of us had anticipated. We were only up the road, and this journey had gone on for 25 minutes and we had gone over a motorway. Something wasn't right, which became very clear when the driver dropped us off. We were back at the ping-pong bar where we had started the night. In his cloudy brain Tim had just selected the address he had seen on the app – assuming that would be our home address. It wasn't, so whereas before we had been 15 minutes' walk from our apartment, we were now an hour away. Tom pleaded with the man to take us to where we lived. I say pleaded; he said some words in no particular order, then informed the man he was having issues with his myocardium (we had googled heart attack in the taxi).

With taxis no longer an option we had to attempt to walk home. I was left in charge of maps (Google, obviously) and the three now zombie-like men walking down the street. I felt like the Pied Piper of Hamelin, except instead of children I had novice drug users, and instead of a pipe I had the promise of water. Trying to get them to follow was like directing smoke; you had no idea what twist or turn would be taken next. The paranoia had set in fully now, one of the three would occasionally scream, 'We're never going to make it!' like we were on some polar exploration mission and not walking down a high street. I was essentially herding geeks: Tom and Tim had started speaking in binary and Steve had taken to picking bits of chewing gum off the ground in the vain hope of getting some sugar in his system. 'Is this sugar-free? Well, it's no help to me!'

Twenty minutes in to our mammoth expedition down Copenhagen's high street, we reached base camp, or 'supermarket', as it's also known. Initially the idea was for us all to go and buy some snacks and drinks, but it soon became very apparent that the bright lights, general population and, in Steve's case, the dairy aisle were too much for my fellow explorers, so I told them to wait outside. However, these clowns couldn't deal with outside either.

Luckily for the lads, European supermarkets have the normal electric sliding doors like we have back home, but also, and possibly due to their love of the 80s, they have kept the push-through gates as well, which leaves a weird no man's land area between the main entrance and the push-through, a sort of supermarket purgatory where you're neither in nor out, perfect for keeping a mat to wipe your feet or three losers who have taken too much weed. So I left the boys in their own personal Upside Down and made my way into the supermarket, but as I walked around and collected a few bits and pieces, I started to realise how not quite with it I was. Compared with three men who had taken roughly 300 per cent more narcotics than was absolutely necessary I had seemed completely coherent. In my head I was basically a young Stephen Fry. Now, however, surrounded by a drug-free population who were all just popping into the supermarket to do their weekly shop, I started to feel a little out of place. I became more and more aware of how I was walking, where I was looking and even how I was standing when picking my Haribo (Tangfastic) – it was all weird and wrong.

I don't know if any of you have ever had that feeling before of being sober enough to know you are acting drunk but far too drunk to do anything about it, the horrible sense of paranoia from the inability to fully control yourself but not being far gone enough to have lost your inhibitions. I don't know if this is just my experience, but there is a weird moment when you're high in which you have a short moment of clarity and look down on yourself, almost like an out-of-body experience, and think, 'What the hell am I doing?'

This moment came to me as I approached the tills and looked over to the no man's land area to see my three friends not saying a word to each other, just standing and staring at entirely different parts of the supermarket. But they seemed unable to stare at any one point for too long, so every three seconds or so they would just randomly change direction, like an insane human timepiece. And because they were so close to the electric doors, every time they moved the doors would slide open, which would trigger another one of Tom's infamous heart attacks. I had my out-of-body experience and thought, 'Oh no, everyone here is going to know that I'm high.' That's when I looked down at my basket and saw that its contents were: Haribo (All Star Mix – I had meant to get Tangfastic), Mars Bar ice creams (it was December in Denmark), hummus, Pringles and WKD Blue. I'd never looked more high in my entire life. I might as well have run into that supermarket screaming 'I HAVE THE MUNCHIES!' I mean, WKD Blue – I love it as much as the next man, but I had picked up seven bottles. Drink all that and you'd get drunk while hearing your teeth dissolve in your head.

We eventually made it back to the apartment and, despite the nightmare of the journey, I managed to have a little moment of victory. I'm glad I got a little reward from the walk back because the problem I find with unrequited acts of kindness is that they are never really given the credit they deserve. If you do something nice for someone it sort of undermines that good deed if you then demand they tell all their friends how amazing you are. Obviously you could tell people yourself, but I'm not becoming that guy, the person who tells everyone how amazing they are over social media. I can't stand those pricks.

'Hey guys, go fund me on my page. I'm doing a skydive for orphans.'

Are you? Or are you just doing a skydive and you want me to pay for it? Anyway, I had my moment in the sun as we approached home and Steve and the Flower Pot Men had to turn to me, thank me and, most importantly, give me the keys to the apartment. Captain Unreliable had reliably guided his troops home and he had the medals (keys) to show for it. I may not be the most reliable man in the world, but at least I can hold my weed and, best of all, none of this needed to find its way onto social media.

CHAPTER 6

NINE TILL FIVE ...

What a Way to Make a Living (Apparently)

Dolly Parton famously sang about this. And I tell you what, she wasn't wrong ... I guess. I myself have never actually been in conventional long-term employment. In my final year at university I found stand-up comedy, and that changed everything. It became really difficult to drag myself into a two-hour lecture on the intricacies of tax law when I was still riding high from making a hundred strangers laugh at some wry observations about my penis the night before. After that, university just started to seem like a bit of a drag – a drag that I had to get up early for. Fuck that. As my attendance dropped, so did my grades, along with my chances of getting a traineeship in the massively competitive world of commercial law – and of getting my bronze attendance certificate.

The problems I encountered will probably sound all too familiar to people around my age. The 'credit crunch' is a piece of terminology I still find offensively coy for the damage it caused. Sort of like calling stabbing someone 'knifey putty inny'. I just feel it doesn't fully encapsulate the destruction it left in its wake. In my specific case it meant that law firms massively cut down on the number of trainees they were taking on, particularly in the commercial sector, which was one of the hardest hit by the credit crunch. On top of this, a number of students who were meant to have started traineeships a year earlier had been paid to defer a year, which, although for them meant a lovely little all-expenses-paid 'gap yah' and disappearing off to some remote land to learn important life lessons like how to make hemp baskets or the best way to let a group of strangers in a cafe know why you're vegan now, it was of very little use to us, the year behind, who had to look on as even more of the already limited places got taken up.

Don't get me wrong, I tried my best to get those jobs. I filled out the applications and answered the questions, questions that managed to be simultaneously bizarre and mundane, which even for a law firm was immensely impressive. I remember being asked on an application form, 'Which three people would you have at your dream dinner party?' Why this is of any relevance in a law-firm job application is genuinely beyond me. Unless of course you answered, 'My three biggest clients, so I could win them on side – I never take a day off.' Actually, that's not bad as far as answers go – you lot can have that for the next job application you do. Although maybe make it slightly more believable, like how about 'My two biggest clients to win them over and Gordon Ramsay to help with snacks'. If that doesn't ingratiate you with the HR team then I've no idea what will. Proper tips for your adult life – you are welcome.

I've never understood that question anyway. If I've got to spend an evening with people, I'd prefer it to be my friends. What am I going to have in common with John Lennon and Winston Churchill? We're just going to be sitting there awkwardly eating gnocchi while they wonder who Alexa is. Also, spending an evening with the great and the good may sound interesting, but inevitably it's just going to make you feel terrible about you own life achievements. 'Oh, you single-handedly changed the course of history, did you, Winston? Well, I have a 4.8 Uber rating.' No, I'd much rather invite people round who make me feel good about my life, like my mates Rick and Greg. Neither of them have been accepted for credits cards yet. Next to them I'm like fucking Gandhi. I really will bang this Gandhi drum until someone starts taking my claim seriously.

When it comes to answering this hypothetical question in a job application, what I can tell you *not* to do is what I did: google 'US presidents', do absolutely fuck-all research and then just pick the one that seemed to get the most press coverage while still remaining (in my eyes, at least) fairly obscure. Clever people pick obscure things – that was my thinking, anyway. So with that in mind I invited to my imaginary dinner party, to impress the HR team at a law firm, Billy Connolly, Charlie Simpson (from Busted) and Richard Nixon. Richard Nixon of Watergate fame. The only president in the history of America to resign from his position, a resignation that came as a result of an almost definitely impending impeachment. The man who illegally bugged the opposition party's phone calls, used questionable and aggressive harassing tactics against activists and had an unpaid tax bill to the tune of roughly half a million dollars. Basically the guy made Donald Trump look like Barney the Dinosaur. I didn't get an interview.

I did work in an office once. It was a long three weeks for everyone concerned. Just me walking about the water cooler screaming wry observations at my colleagues.

'How weird was it when a dog got into the school playground?'

'Have you every tried a cannabis cookie?'

'My mate's baby is a racist arsehole!'

'That's lovely, Iain. Now please go back to your cubical – you've upset Pete from accounts.'

My very specific set of skills was hugely underappreciated within the confines of the office environment. I need space for my ideas to fly. Also, early mornings are not my thing. Like, not my thing at all. Sometimes people say to me, 'Oh, Iain, I'm not a morning person either,' and to them I reply, 'Have you ever slept in for a gig that starts at 8 p.m.?' If I'm honest, I started stand-up 10 per cent for the artistic outlet it afforded me, 10 per cent thanks to my unhealthy need for unquestioned attention from strangers, and 80 per cent for the lie-ins. I love a lie-in so, so much. I'm addicted. My love of the lie-in means I've been roughly 30 minutes late for every appointment I've ever had. Morning routines are streamlined in order to maximise lie-in potential. A 50-minute morning routine of breakfast, shower, get dressed and podcast download (for journey) can be reduced to: 45 minutes in bed, look at watch, scream obscenities, find fresh pants and some mouthwash then bolt out the house – where I will undoubtedly have forgotten my headphones.

As I mentioned earlier, I recently performed at the Melbourne International Comedy Festival, which is the world's largest comedy-dedicated festival. Or a massive piss-up in the sunshine depending on how comfortable you are with Australia's alcohol-pricing policy. Seven pounds a pint? Come on, lads, it's boiling here – can we please have a cheaper option for us sunburnt Brits? In Australia a lot of their successful comics make the move over to breakfast radio. That's what Australian comedians choose to do – they get a job that requires them to be in a studio between the hours of six and ten in the morning! Who in their right mind would do that to themselves? I couldn't do breakfast radio. Everything about it sickens me. Early mornings, five days a week, for the rest of time ... I would eventually go insane.

Breakfast radio with me at the helm would be a very different experience for everyone concerned: 'Good morning, everyone. It's 6.23 a.m. and today's text-in is this – it's before 10 a.m. and you're up. What the fuck is wrong with you people?' I always assume a breakfast-radio host is asleep in between tracks, and the producer's primary job is to belt them with a stick (or perhaps an old school cane) a few seconds before the end, just in time for them to wake up and introduce the traffic.

I know my hatred of the early morning isn't an opinion held by everyone, as I now have people in my life who do insane things in the mornings. I have got friends, people I actually know and trust, who do stuff before work. Did you get that? *Before* work. Like, *after* sleep and *before* work they're running around carrying out duties and achieving goals. After sleep and before work? How is anyone fitting anything into that five-minute window? I struggle to find a clean pair of pants. I know people who go to the gym *before work*. You don't go to the gym before work, you sleep in so long that you have to skip the shower you so badly need and question your life decisions, have a little cry and then you go to work. Not these maniacs. Off to the gym they go, to hang out with those weird, monstrous-looking lads who hang out in the free-weights room slowly losing their personality as well as their own neck. I don't want to bump into these guys at the best of times, let alone pre-lunch.

'Yo, bro, what do you lift?'

'Yes I do, as it goes. I can lift the mood, by asking you to leave.'

Not only do these 'before work' animals openly embrace all these horrific events and characters, but thanks to social media they can now openly broadcast this insane behaviour to the entire world, like it's some historical news event. And, as we've already discussed, boy, do our generation love to perform, and the 'before work' crew are the smuggest of the lot. Coming from a millennial that is saying a lot. They pop up in your Insta stories, walking down the street, in public, speaking into their phones like it's the most normal thing in the entire world. I never trust anyone with that level of confidence. I couldn't record myself on a phone in a public space. I'm blown away by anyone who can enter a room filled with strangers and not forget how to walk properly. But there they are, bouncing down the street with the time clearly plastered on the front of the video while they mutter the most bizarre nonsense: 'Hey, guys. Funday Monday. I've had such a mad busy weekend. Like, Sunday night I spent the whole evening putting all my meals for this week in Tupperware.' Oh please, just fuck off.

I met these 'before work' psychopaths during my short but eventful stint in an office. They will approach you at any given opportunity, the question burning deep inside them. They won't even walk; the high levels of optimism in their bodies allow them to float towards you, happiness dripping off them like the grease that drips from the elephant leg that rotates slowly in your local kebab shop. Then the question comes flying out: 'Hey there, Iain. Have you been up to much before work?'

Piss off, Karen, you can tell I've not showered. I'm eating cereal off the keyboard. Fuck all has happened before work. Do you know what I did this morning? I microwaved my McDonald's from the night before. It was still in the brown bag, Karen. Do you know why? Let me tell you. The brown bag had been rolled shut and I was so hungover I looked at that brown bag and thought to myself, 'I cannot solve this puzzle right now – this brown Rubik's Cube.' I love everything about McDonald's: the colours, the ambience, *everything*. Believe me that love is real, it's 100 per cent my favourite restaurant in the world. And yes, it is a restaurant.

THE SQUADDIE GIG FUCK-UP (PART I)

My relationship with any form of work has always been, how do you say, more eventful than I would have liked. A fair few years ago I was asked to do one of my first ever corporate gigs. For those unfamiliar with the concept, a corporate gig is where a comedian is asked to perform at a company's Christmas do or awards ceremony – if you're really lucky you get to host a whole conference and sit through an entire working day's worth of rubbish in-jokes and meaningless corporate jargon. If you're struggling to picture that, it normally goes something like: 'This quarter was a really unpredictable time for our over-heads; luckily the sales team pulled through with some great figures in the back to really bolster our gross takings. Speaking of gross, do you all remember how *gross* it was when Craig in marketing threw up everywhere after those Jägerbombs at our financial ball last year? That guy is jokes!'

So, as you can imagine, the offer of corporate gig fills us comedians with a sense of dread reserved normally for Ronald McDonald at a vegan music festival. However, the money is bloody fantastic so on goes the suit, out goes the artistic integrity and off to the corporate you trot, armed with hastily writ-ten 'in-jokes' thanks to the company's website.

The reason these events are such well-paid affairs boils down to how tricky they are to play. Normally this is a group of 200-plus people who all spend a year working together and developing friendships in a professional capacity, and once a year they get to dress up, drink heavily and catch up with everyone they fail to see properly the rest of the year because they are all too busy 'hitting targets' or 'securing sustainable income revenues for the business'. So you can imagine the pandemonium when they are all put in a fun, informal environment together. Imagine a Hollywood reconstruction of a prom night. Like, a full-blown *A Cinderella Story*, expensive-looking affair. But instead of school children you get a load of overworked bankers, and instead of some innocent fruit-based punch it's gallons of free booze paid for by the company bosses, who have one night to distract everyone from the fact that they're on 10 times the salary of anyone else in the room and convince them that they are still, amazingly, 'one of the people'.

And just think how keen you'd be, when you're getting drunk with friends for the first time in ages, to sit quietly and pay attention to a comedian you've never heard of. As a comedian you walk onto that stage, full of drunk, chatty people who are enjoying the biggest night out of their year, and ask them to listen to jokes about the time you had a 'crazy' experience on a bus or told an eight-year-old to go fuck himself. It very rarely, if ever, goes well. Corporate people still book more comedians regardless, and we keep showing up and dying. And so the awful artist–corporate dance continues, until the planet runs out of resources and global Armageddon breaks out in which neither bankers nor comedians will have much to offer the new global wasteland, and as a result are among the first of the groups to be eaten. But like I've said before, boy, do they pay well.

This particular corporate was up in the north of England, quite the drive for a little London dweller such as myself. Now, to some of the Scottish contingent reading this, I can hear you screaming at me, 'How dare you call yourself a London dweller – you're Scottish, how dare you identify with those English heathens!' And the simple answer to that is I don't really buy into the whole England vs Scotland horseshit, and to those who think I'm being unpatriotic, let me tell you this. The reason I don't buy into any of that is for the simple reason that I know Scotland's better. I don't feel the need to keep up this pointless competition – we've won, go easy on my little English buddies. And to the English reading this who are thinking of stopping now owing to that rather hearty 'slam', don't worry, your fellow countrymen and women at this particular corporate gig are about to redress the balance – so do read on. And to my Welsh and Irish brothers and sisters, sorry you had to witness this bickering.

Anyway, I arrived at the venue, which I will call 'The North' for legal reasons, for my delightful corporate gig, with a couple of factors affecting my dreams of having a peaceful gig and returning home unscathed. First, this gig was very near Christmas. Obviously I knew it was close to Christmas before I got there – I had been operating off the Christian calendar for well over 20 years at this point. But it was so close to Christmas that this particular gig was being called a 'Christmas party'. A Christmas party where the audience would be full of Christmas goodwill, and by Christmas goodwill I do mean Jägerbombs. It's a very British thing that, getting absolutely muntered during religious festivals. I'm shocked that there aren't more reports of little British grannies walking up to the pulpit during Sunday communion, grabbing the bottle of communion wine, downing the whole thing and screaming at those taking the body of Christ, 'Eating's cheating ... Another round of Jesus Blood, please, Father!' Second, this gig wasn't for any corporate suits – it was for a group of squaddies who were enjoying a spot of Christmas dinner before they headed off to take part in whatever war was taking place. This was their war warm-up. This might be rough.

I arrived at the gig with Canadian comedian Craig Campbell. The only reason I mention Craig's North American heritage is because the man is about as stereotypical a Canadian as you can get, and as you may have ascertained through the Antigua anecdote earlier, in particular my grandmother's height, I do love a bit of visual imagery to help the reader along. Craig is tall, and his long hair and beard smell incredible, much better than their dishevelled appearance would suggest. He owns limitless biker gear, which is worn at all times, including while he is on stage, and this isn't because it's now on trend and available from Topman, but rather because he drives a fucking motorbike, and when I say fucking motorbike, I mean *fucking* motorbike. The sort of bike suggesting that, were a lady to take a seat on it, she would instantly get pregnant. He talks about hiking and lumber and isn't scared of anyone or anything. But remember he's Canadian, so he's all that but still the nicest man you can imagine: looks like a grizzly bear, sounds like Justin Trudeau's loveable uncle. Basically Craig is, in modern tongue, 'an absolute legend'. But he did ask me to stop smelling his beard.

Craig and I walked into the large hotel function room, which felt and looked more like a working-men's club than I could ever have imagined a hotel function room looking. It was almost like the working-men's club had done so well they had decided to pop a bunch of rooms in the back to cater for the sudden increase in attendance. At one end of the room, which was easily five or six football pitches in size, sat the bar, which was manned by four bar staff who were noticeably stressed at being behind a bar that was straining under the weight of the men shoving themselves up against it, men who were nearly as pissed as they were massive. The bar queue was easily six or seven deep and the same again wide with these behemoths shouting things like 'Hurry up, love,' 'I've more chance of getting a drink in Afghanistan' and 'Fuck it, I'll just buy a bottle of vodka – it'll be quicker.'

More worrying than that – and who knew that something could be more worrying than a modern-day warrior ordering a bottle of Glen's – was the other end of the room, where there was a large raised stage, upon which stood a rock band who were playing all the classics – think an uncle's 50th, but louder. The worry wasn't the band – although, as a spoken-word artist (which is what stand-up is – fuck you!), it's not an ideal act to follow – the real fear came from the indifference in the room. To be clear, unlike an uncle's 50th there was no dancing, no kids running across the dance floor then sliding on their knees, no nothing. They didn't even listen to the music. Not only were the squaddies not listening to the band, but they were trying to speak over the intrusive music that was damaging their precious catch-up time. That's right, I was going to perform comedy to a bunch of pissed-up soldiers who were capable of talking louder than a Marshall speaker stack. This wasn't looking good. Not good at all.

YOU'RE ON YOUR OWN

This gig was the first where I'd truly felt out of my comfort zone. The novelty of doing stand-up as my profession had melted away and the harsh reality of what I had to do to pay the rent became very real. I would have to deal with this whole situation all on my own. I couldn't get my mum to call in sick for me – something I asked her to do well into my twenties, which still makes me shudder with shame at least once a month. There was no school initiative built into the gig so the squaddies would give me one of their infamous army medals for being brave and 'trying my best', despite the far from ideal conditions that lay before me. Obviously I am not comparing this gig to the horrors of war. That would be insensitive. Insensitive to me – this was far worse than war. Those guys had guns during war, I just had anecdotes and a wireless microphone. I was just going to have to get on with it, by myself, and face the consequences.

The worst bit is that I was 25 at the time. I'd had my first break-up, but in that situation I had my parents and friends to hold my hand through the painful experience. How had I managed to get so far down the line without ever having to face failure on my own before? The answer is because the people and institutions that cared for me protected me from it. But I was starting to learn, really bloody quickly, that maybe it wasn't the best way to have gone about things.

'THE MILLENNIAL QUESTION'

In a very famous internet clip called 'The Millennial Question', Simon Sinek talks about the four main factors that he feels lead to millennials failing to integrate into the working world. I really recommend you give it a watch, if you haven't already. I mean, a few years ago the clip was all over Facebook! I suppose if you haven't seen it, well done you. Maybe your social-media addiction isn't as bad as we first feared.

So onto Simon's brilliantly formed, four-part argument. Why is it we millennials, we fragile little snowflakes, struggle so much when introduced to the world of work? Simon states (which is kind of like 'Simon Says', but rather than following basic instructions you just listen to a shitload of TED Talks) that, on top of 'bad parenting models' and technology, you add a feeling of impatience. We now live in a world in which you can binge-watch your favourite TV series in a day at the click of a button, and you don't even need to sit through the advertisements. Dating no longer involves awkward conversations or meeting the scary dads at the front door as you collect your partner from their house on your way to the cinema. Now you swipe right, and BANG! You're a digital Casanova.

This need for immediacy doesn't help us in the real world, however, because, as Simon states, there are certain things that don't have shortcuts – such as love and job fulfilment. But this is hard to comprehend for someone who's grown up on YouTube clips, funny memes and the phenomenal Domino's Pizza app. This lack of immediacy within a working environment leaves us feeling like we aren't making an 'impact' at work – even though we might only have been there a matter of weeks. Job satisfaction can be a long and arduous journey, something we have very little experience of. This brings us onto Simon's final point, that of environment. One of the biggest issues facing corporations now is that they are taking on millennials, with all our faults and issues, and airdropping us into environments that care more about the bottom line of the corporation than the actual humans working within them, a model that goes back to the 1980s, the first decade in which lay-offs and redundancies were used in order to 'balance the books'. Businesses haven't changed much since then, except Domino's Pizza, who, as I've already said, have done wonderful things with their app.

This isn't a question of companies taking on the role of the parent, which the millennial misses so greatly; it's simply about empathy. Yes, as a generation we need to start taking responsibility for our own actions and emotions, but if you understand why your workforce feel and behave a certain way then you can help them improve not only for themselves, but as employees. A happy workforce is a productive workforce. It sounds twee but it's true. Companies need to teach their new employees the benefits of long-term work and achievement. Teach people that, and the whole company will benefit – not just millennials.

THE SQUADDIE GIG FUCK-UP (PART II)

Having watched 300 squaddies completely ignore the rock band's big closing rendition of Queen's 'Bohemian Rhapsody', Craig and I retired to his hotel room to discuss the game plan, knowing we were the next thing on the entertainment list. There are two things I remember very vividly from that chat. The first is how manly the room smelt. Do you know when a proper man has been in a room and it just smells like, well, *man*? The sort of smell that suggests the room's shelves have definitely been put up properly and there is 100 per cent an AA road map within reaching distance. My rooms never smell like that, largely because I'm not particularly manly and I fucking love a scented candle.

204

My second vivid memory is that I was absolutely shitting myself, and this isn't some strategically employed hyperbole. I could not be more serious. For the first time in my life I genuinely felt that a little bit of poo could actually come out. Like I was some sort of exotic frog, except instead of excreting a deadly venom to ward off predators, I would just slightly soil my brand new pair of CKs. That'll show them!

Unbelievably, Craig did not share my guttural fear of our impending doom. He'd done this all before: he had smashed gigs, had tough gigs, been cheered, booed and everything in between. Basically, he had life experience. Sure, I had been stabbed once, but that wasn't enough. Craig was acting like this was just the most normal thing in the entire world. It isn't, mate. This isn't normal. These animals are going to eat us alive. They're louder than Marshall speaker stacks. Admittedly, Craig grew up in Canada and so is used to being around things that want to kill you, and, to be fair to him, he does look like the sort of man who could not only survive a brutal bear attack, but would probably force the beast to send him a full written apology after the event. So despite my protestations he assured me that we should go ahead with the gig and things were going to be absolutely fine. That was the position we both held for a further two peaceful minutes until news arrived that was to send the whole event into a severe nose-dive.

The promoter of the 'gig' – as we were still optimistically calling it – came into our room to alert us to a small piece of information he felt was rather pertinent to our performance. Now, in the world of corporate entertainment this sort of thing isn't unusual. More often than not the people running the event will have a long list of things you can and cannot say. Because although they always ensure us that they are a 'great bunch of people who are 100 per cent up for a laugh', there is similarly a bunch of things you shouldn't say because you might offend someone important and then not get paid, which for these sorts of gigs is the worst outcome imaginable.

However, this run-of-the-mill pep talk was not your usual 'our sponsors are on tables four and seven, and under no circumstances make fun of them in any way!' This was far, far worse, and even sent the unflappable Canadian man mountain into a crisis of confidence: 'Sorry, guys, but I've just been speaking to some of the lads and, although I have no idea where this has come from, it appears they are under the belief that performing tonight is Al Murray the Pub Landlord.'

Al Murray, I know him well. He is a lovely man and do you know what else he is? Incredibly popular with the armed forces. Do you know who isn't popular with the armed forces? The peculiar mix of a 25-year-old who looks like a rejected member of McFly and an eccentric lumberjack. If we were to go on stage without these men being made aware of the change in personnel then there would be war ... literally. Even Craig's confident exterior had crumbled; at one point he checked the trouser leg of his biking leathers, presumably to see if any poo had started to dribble out. The three of us stuck our heads together and came up with a plan that would hopefully help us out of the massive Al Murray-shaped hole we currently found ourselves in. Would it work? Well, we were about to find out.

FINDING YOUR 'WHY'

People often think that stand-up comedy is a very glamorous existence, a world of showbiz and celebrity, but the reality is it's more like rooms above pubs and missed social functions. The amount of birthdays and weddings I've missed because I've had to drive to provincial towns I've never heard of to perform to an uninterested audience who seem completely unmoved by the fact that I've given up *another* Saturday to be with them.

Even getting an audience together can be a tricky task. Long before the *Love Island* juggernaut took off I would tour the counties with my shows. Once I went to Exeter and three people showed up. Now, don't get me wrong, they were lovely people, they just weren't enough people. The real issue arose when the audience collectively decided that they needed the toilet. Well, not collectively. The couple decided they needed the toilet and then the man who had shown up on his own asked to leave with them. And to be fair to the guy, without the couple in the room this gig was precariously close to becoming a lap dance. I don't know if you've been to a gig where the entire audience have to go to the toilet, but when they do, the performer just has to wait. Standing on stage, lights on and mic still live, waiting. Longest five minutes of my life just standing there thinking, 'Have they gone for a shit or have they just left?' I missed my best friend's 30th for that gig. Showbiz, eh?

I often have people ask me if I was 'the funny one at school' or 'the joker in the family'. The truth is that comedians aren't necessarily the funniest people in the room (although that undoubtedly does help), but they are the people who need it the most. The truth is stand-up is hard work. It's lonely, as you lose contact with friends and family due to unsociable work schedules. A comedian, whose name annoyingly slips my mind, once described doing stand-up as 'you get paid for the eight hours' driving then go and do a gig for free'.

None of that matters, however, because when it goes right, there is nothing like it. That moment you go on stage and get a laugh, it's like a drug. No, forget that, it's better than drugs. After performing comedy I've never woken up in the afternoon on a massive comedown, slowly realising that the night before I texted my ex five times to tell her I loved her. For me at least, on that stage, in that moment, everything makes sense – there isn't a worry in the world. Well, sometimes you worry why no one's laughing, or if that hen do on the front row will ever stop talking – once I worried about whether I'd locked my front door – but you get the idea! Stand-up is my happiness. If I had to define happiness it would be that: doing what you love, for no other reason than you want to do it. Completely in the moment, no thought of future plans, career trajectory or what anyone else makes of it. If there is a drug better than that then get me a box of it, please. Like I've said, I haven't done many drugs – do they come in boxes? A very good comedian, better friend and former flatmate once described stand-up comedy perfectly: 'Most people have a job they don't necessarily like in order to have an enjoyable social life, whereas comedians have given up on their social life in order to have a job they love.'

American stand-up and personal hero of mine Bill Burr once told a story on his podcast about his time in New York. Comfortably in his 30s, completely skint and sleeping in his friend's flat on a pull-out couch, his life at that point was essentially the start of a Judd Apatow movie. You can see the out-of-work comedian being played by Seth Rogan, and the rest writes itself. That night he had been booked to do a new-material night, in which he could try out new jokes and ideas, and the audience paid less for a ticket knowing that the quality might be varied. New jokes are like babies – some are wonderful things and others are fucking awful. That night Bill went to his new-material gig, tried out some new jokes and received $30 in payment. The gig went well, he had a few beers with fellow comics after the gig and headed home. He sat on his pull-out couch so happy that his new jokes had gone down well. He then spotted his friend and, technically speaking, landlord looking rather upset. He asked her what was wrong and she replied, 'I wish I had a job where I could give up an evening for $30 and be as happy as you about it.' That obviously isn't a word-for-word retelling of the story, but the sentiment really spoke to me. Why was Bill so satisfied as he sat on a pull-out couch while the woman who owned that apartment felt so flat and unfulfilled?

Simon Sinek – he's back again, the clever sod – states that companies (and for my purposes, individuals) need to find their 'why'. He says that corporations tend to work out *what* they do, *how* they do it and *why* they do it – normally in that order. However, he argues that if you work out 'why' you do something first, you are more likely to increase customer and employee retention. Sinek repeats a sort of mantra several times during his TED Talk 'Find Your Why': 'People don't buy what you do; they buy why you do it.'

I think this 'why' is what many of us lack in our lives today. Growing up, we were told that we were special, we could achieve anything, and then all of a sudden the credit crunch happened and the whole environment changed. Our desire to 'be the best' and to 'do what we love' stopped being seen as aspirational and instead was interpreted as being spoilt brats that 'expected too much'. 'Why do you lot expect so much?' the older generation would constantly ask. BECAUSE YOU FUCK-ING TOLD ME! YOU TOLD ME I COULD BE AN ASTRONAUT – YOU SAID!

Instead of this dream of perfection we were promised, we enter jobs in order to survive, in order to earn, and rather than strive to improve, we are told we should be grateful for it, happy with our lot – because times are tough and jobs are hard to come by. There seems to be little focus on what we hope to achieve and learn from our employment, despite the fact that work will account for 40 hours of our week for the rest of our lives. To really commit to something that engulfs so much of your time you need to feel that the activity has a common purpose and, more importantly, that you are contributing to that common purpose in a significant way.

So with business seemingly having no interest outside their profit margins, a far from ideal environment for millennials to thrive in, they will very rarely focus on their 'why', and as a result fail to give their workforce a common purpose to unite and motivate everyone within that business. Maybe I wouldn't have shunned the conventional working environment so early in my life if I'd found a workplace where everyone followed the same goals and passions, going into work everyday with a group of people who all shared the same common purpose. Actually, fuck that, you have to get up early – I'm out.

So why do we millennials, apparently the vainest generation ever to grace God's green earth, put up with these unfulfilling jobs today? Why don't we all just leave our nine to fives and run off on our thirteenth gap year? I mean, this time we could blog the whole thing! Think of the things you could achieve without the shackles of employment. You could open your own vegan cafe in your home town's latest up-and-coming hotspot. A cafe in which artists, who previously had to suffer the inhumane conditions of a Starbucks, could now work on their latest short film while getting stuck in to a delicious matcha latte with almond milk. Sounds absolutely lovely, right? Who wouldn't want to live their life like that? Free to do and say whatever you like. Live life by your own rules, being your own boss, paying an acceptable level of tax – it's the fucking dream, I tell thee! So why would a generation who were told en masse that they were precious little flowers who could achieve anything they put their minds to not take up this dream of living in a boss-free, hipster utopia? Why do we find ourselves in the daily nine-to-five grind every single Monday through Friday, having to save our drainpipe jeans, part-time poetry and cocktails served out of tea pots for the weekend? Be a comedian like me. Saturdays can be a drag, but you can't beat getting pissed on a Tuesday. Pubs are nice and empty. Result.

WE'RE ALL SKINT, BRUV!

Since the financial crisis of 2007 one of the main reasons for millennials failing to find fulfilment though work is money. Or, to put it another way, we're all skint, bruv! I was at university when the crash happened, and the change in the way students were spoken to regarding employment was marked. At Edinburgh University Law School, for the first year or so, lecturers would speak to us about our future job prospects with a level of arrogance a student of today would barely recognise. The stench of smug billowing out of the halls following career meetings was incredible.

'But you go to Edinburgh University, so that shouldn't be an issue' was the catchphrase wheeled out in answer to the possible problems facing post-graduates of the day. However, after the crash things changed in what felt like 24 hours. 'Grab any job you can get your grubby little student claws on!' they would scream. I mean, not quite, but you get the idea. Edinburgh University computers saw their Edinburgh-

University-crest-embossed mouse mats replaced with mats advertising middle-management, post-grad positions in places like Aldi, Costco and every bank you could ever think of. Not that there is anything wrong with any of those places of work, but it wasn't the dream we Edinburgh law graduates were sold when we applied. We weren't meant to have any issues. We expected to stroll into the best careers the world had to offer. But why? Why would you think that, you self-entitled egomaniacs? Why? Because, and I cannot make this point clear enough, because you told us – you fucking said!

We fail to see work as a place to achieve life satisfaction, and instead see it as simply a way to make money and put food on the table. I mean, don't get me wrong, this is a really important thing – I love having food on my table. Best place for food, if you ask me. A few times as a student I was so skint that the food I wanted on the table had to stay on a supermarket shelf, and that sucked. When the only food on your table is rice, you really appreciate the importance of work than can result in something a little more substantial, like a taco kit. The family in the advert always look so happy

Those of our generation who go on to university feel they are married to the work they can get as a result of all that blood, sweat and tears sacrificed in the name of their degree. No one wants to spend five years and 40 grand studying maths, and then go off and get a job that doesn't utilise numbers. Maths is fucking hard – you're not going to buy set squares every year, learn how to spell parallelogram and study all the number stuff just so you can then go off and be a chef. What would be the point in that? They have no crossover at all. Well, they both use pie and you could possibly use one of your rulers as a spatula, but that's about it. I mean, I studied law and then spent my first four years of employment talking to a puppet dog, but I feel like I'm something of an exception to the rule. I mean, it was either the fantastical world of children's TV or Aldi, and CBBC had the cooler mouse mats. Tracy Beaker ones, to be exact. What an absolute treat!

Our fear of failure – or at least failing to succeed quickly – means millennials are scared to walk away from something in which they've invested heavily. To change career paths years into it feels like a massive step backwards and delays the speed at which we can start to achieve and thrive. No one wants to start again at 30. You'll be 40 by the time you get anywhere in life, and who wants that? You'll be all grey and wrinkly. Well, some folk still look great, even at 50, like Jared Leto or Kylie Minogue, but everyone knows they're freaks of nature. Or spent a fortune on cosmetic surgery, one or the other. I don't know, I'm not a doctor – I'm a lawyer. Well, I nearly was. Anyway, we're getting off topic. You must be successful by 30, tops, or you might as well be dead.

Another challenge for the Facebook generation is the light relief social media offers us. A little pressure valve that can stop the daily grind becoming all too much. Obviously, this is not an entirely bad thing – a bit of light relief can often be good. I remember when I was younger and Stacey dumped me over MSN Messenger and I was so sad. I mean, properly upset. I was alone as well when it happened, which adds real depth to the sadness. There is something about being sad and alone that really allows you to access your guttural angst. Away I went crying, and I cried like I'd never cried before until outside I saw a squirrel humping the living shit out of a garden gnome. His genitals were aimed at the old gnome's head too, which made it look like they were sixty-nining. From another angle it looked like the squirrel had a massive green hat coming out of its anus. From up top you could see that the cheeky little gnome still had a massive smile on his face, the dirty bastard! I looked at a squirrel's balls slap off the porce-lain face of an imaginary being and started laughing my arse off. I learnt an important life lesson that day – light relief can be a good thing.

The problem with social media, however, is that the relief might be slight but it's constant, not the infrequent pick-me-up you get from day-to-day life but an ever-present numbing buzz. With this emotionally numbing technology at our finger-tips it lessens our drive to improve. When you are unhappy with your weight a few choice camera angles and spot of clever photo editing will make your Insta 'pop' – lessening your drive to lose a few pounds, or indeed coming to terms with your current weight, whatever works for you. Similarly, the constant bings and bongs of any social platform can result in you endur-ing a work environment that you otherwise would have left years ago; social media means you can seek approval from your peers through getting 'likes' or messages of support so you don't feel as strong an urge to improve your current situa-tion – the satisfaction is derived elsewhere.

Social media very rarely makes anyone feel true happiness: no digital experience will ever come close to witnessing a squirrel tea-bagging a garden ornament; it just leaves us feeling constantly dis-satisfied all the time, monitoring our unhappiness rather than actually solving it, sort of like a shot of insulin for the soul. Having everyone you've ever met in your pocket means you are never truly alone. Without that real sense of solitude you're never in a position where you feel like you can just have a proper cry – or at least a half-decent wank.

THE SQUADDIE GIG FUCK-UP (PART III)

Back 'up north', the possibility of a depressingly mundane existence was very far down my list of worries. Craig, the booker and I had finalised our plan to survive what was becoming an increasingly worrying ordeal for everyone concerned. The plan was simple: we would speak to the head squaddie, the squaddie king, if you will, and get him to alert his fellow troops of the change in entertainment personnel. Surely the soldiers would accept the news coming from their leader – they were men and women who would follow him into battle, after all. He might even get them to listen and laugh – this gig might not be the disaster we all first thought! There was a pang of excitement running through me, and it wasn't due to a Facebook 'like'.

That excitement quickly turned to despair when we met the king of the squaddies, a man who not only was the most important person in the room, but easily the most drunk. I wish I could tell you his name, but when we asked him for it he drunkenly slurred something about 'that's none of your business' and then something about my slightly longish hair and what would happen to me in prison. Long story short, I'm fucked if I know what this dude was called. Despite this, we passed on the information about the booking error, introduced ourselves and asked politely if he would do the same to the crowd. He burped, threw up in his mouth a bit and then kindly agreed to do it. We walked back through to the hotel function room cum working-men's club to see that in the 40 minutes we had been backstage, seven hours of drinking had somehow taken place. The place had gone well and truly feral. I looked to Craig and asked him if we should even go ahead with this absolute disaster of a gig, begging him with my eyes to say no. He didn't give a fuck, though. He'd done this all before. He was ready to be mauled by bears.

The squaddie king walked onto the stage to welcome me and rally the troops (quite literally). As he got up there the crowd erupted. It was like nothing I'd seen before – well, it was kind of like Michael McIntyre walking out at Wembley, but I'd only seen that on DVD and I didn't recall hearing 300 men chanting 'You fucking legend' as he approached the microphone. As the squaddie king took the microphone he began to address the troops, and quiet fell over the room – a silence that was swiftly dealt with. He went to clear his throat, threw up in

217

his mouth again slightly, then proceeded to scream down the mic: 'OI, OI!'

The whole room responded instantaneously in almost perfect unison. This call and response continued for a solid five minutes. So long, in fact, that the squaddie king had actually forgotten everything we'd previously discussed, like alerting the troops to the lack of Al Murray. He'd even managed to forget my name, so instead he introduced me by simply stating: 'Ladies and gentlemen, please welcome to the stage ... a boy.'

So out I walked to 300 trained killers wearing looks of confusion and anger. Instead of their hero Al Murray they had a kid telling jokes about how weird it is being friends with your mum on Facebook. Understandably, they didn't take to my musings on millennial life. Also, you probably won't be surprised to learn that it's hard to tell an audience 'a mental thing happened to me the other day' when the entire audience have been to war, many on more than one occasion. They've been shot at, with actual guns, and I'm trying to tell them about a time someone said something nasty to me on the bus. After a few more minutes of abject silence, the chatting began. At first in small isolated pockets around the room, before descending into a very clear hum that filled the hotel function room cum working-men's club cum comedy club cum pub. I wish that was as bad as it got.

At this point in my comedy career I hadn't experienced much failure. I had entered a few competitions and done fairly well, and most of my gigs had been very studenty, so the crowds were mostly supportive and around my age. This was a real change. A life hitherto shielded from failure had not set me up to be in a massive room, 300 yards away from an audience that didn't want to listen to what I had to say. For years I had been led to believe that what I had to say was important. But eventually you grow up and realise that people don't give a shit what you think. That's the hole social media is trying to fill, the need we all have for what we say and do to be of some importance to someone. Sometimes it isn't and that's fine. Sometimes it's fine to do or say something just for you. That's why Craig was so relaxed. It wasn't because he had gigged all over the world, lived a long life and possibly (in my mind) killed a bear; it was because he knew that it didn't matter if, on this occasion, people didn't like or want to hear what he had to say. Tonight was work, and tomorrow it wouldn't matter. I think that's a really important lesson to learn – one I would have preferred not to in front of hundreds of the scariest and drunkest individuals I had ever met in my life.

As I stared at the crowd, far away and becoming less interested in me and more consumed by their personal conversations, I racked my brain for my next move. Why didn't they want to listen? I decided that it wasn't the absence of Al Murray, it wasn't the alcohol consumed or the fact that they only had tonight left before the harsh realities of warfare became their primary concern. It was the distance. That was it! I was too far from my people, so I came up with a cunning plan. I removed the wireless hand-held mic from its stand, jumped off the stage and walked towards the crowd, who had by now all but erased me from their night out.

As I walked towards them I became aware of another fact that had escaped me until now, about the truly artificial nature of stand-up comedy. With the raised stage, the lighting and the audience facing in your direction, the whole concept of stand-up is an easy pill to swallow. When you take that away, however, you no longer have a stand-up comedian. Instead you have 'a boy' who was bothering the army. Thanks to the microphone I still had some authority, but an amplified nuisance is still a nuisance in anyone's eyes. I decided to go table by table, 'bantering' with the revellers individually. I know, don't worry – that uncomfortable feeling you're now enjoying is the same I experience every time I tell this story. The demographic of the room hardly lent itself to much comedic banter.

'What do you do?'

'The army.'

'What do you do?'

'The army.'

'What do you do?'

'An analyst.'

'Oh, really? What do you analyse?'

'The army.'

Damn it! This continued for a further five minutes before one of the squaddies approached me. Now, to say this lad was massive would have been an understatement. To give you an idea of his intimidating presence I would say that he was *definitely* ginger, but I would bet my house that no one had ever mentioned this to him. Basically he looked like someone had shaved a bear, got it drunk and given it camouflage. Craig would have had a field day! The man in question – 'Daz', I believe his name was – made his way towards me, shouting and balling. The room was so loud that I couldn't make out the drunken screams, but as he got nearer I could hear them quite clearly. In fact, he was so near by now that as well as shouting, he was also trying to prise the microphone from my hand: 'You're shite! Get off the stage – you're shite!'

Despite the string of terrible decisions I had made up to that point, I did manage to resist the temptation to correct his factually incorrect heckle by shouting back at him, 'I'm not even on stage!' and then running off giggling like a teenager. Instead I gave our good friend Daz a challenge. I looked him right in his face, which had gone a weird purple colour owing to the screaming, and said, 'I bet you can't do 10 push-ups with me on your back.'

To this day I don't fully understand why these words left my lips. I'm guessing it had something to do with me going through a Filofax of activities that alpha males enjoy and randomly landing on 'gym'. Lads love the gym, so let's do some gym. Amazingly, it worked. Daz got down into the push-up position and a hush fell over the room. 'It's working!' I thought to myself. 'It's actually fucking working!' The bear/Daz then stood up and made an announcement over the microphone that he had, unsurprisingly, managed to prise from my beta-male grip: 'This will actually work a lot better if you lie underneath and sort of cradle on.'

Now, a lot of you might have already guessed that the gym is not my forte, so I was unfamiliar with the logistics of the

221

two-man push-up, which is the main reason why what happened next happened. Much to Daz's confusion and delight, I obediently lay on the floor. After a few seconds of eager anticipation from everyone in the room, Daz proceeded to leap on top of me and vigorously dry-hump me. He was there for so long that at one point a bead of sweat dripped off his forehead and plopped perfectly into my mouth. It tasted like testosterone and real ale. I can only drink lager now. The crowd understandably lost their minds. They erupted – like, properly went mad. I finally had my Michael McIntyre moment, and I'm sure even Michael would admit that the spectacle I created that evening was funnier than anything he had managed in his lengthy and impressive career. This was my 'man drawer'. After a few seconds or so the chanting started. Unfortunately no one in the audience knew my name, so they were all just shouting, in unison: 'FUCK. THE. BOY. FUCK. THE. BOY. FUCK. THE BOY.'

I looked over to Craig, my elder, my confidant, my fellow artiste. Surely he would come to my aid? He'd been here before, he knew how to tame even the most unruly of bears. Unfortunately, Craig would not help me that night, as he was too busy pissing himself laughing while filming the whole thing on his mobile phone. Months later Craig and I would be taken into a room at our management's office and be told that the promoter had failed to pay us and subsequently moved to Australia, making it difficult to track him down. We were told that the only way we could get the money back would be legal action, which would be pricey and possibly fruitless. We decided not to pursue it. I asked Craig a few years later if he still had the footage; he said it was probably on an old phone somewhere, but was unsure of its exact whereabouts. I told him not to worry, I barely even think about it now ...

That night I learnt a number of important lessons: 1) It's absolutely fine for people not to take an interest in what you've got to say all the time, 2) don't lie down in front of a drunken alpha male, and 3) never trust a Canadian. These lessons have all continued to help me achieve my 'why' of becoming the best stand-up I can be. So long as I continue to strive to improve as a comedian I hope that will always be enough to keep me happy. Don't get me wrong, I love being paid – that whole 'food on the table' thing really cannot be overlooked, it really is a fucking treat. But you need to achieve that by doing something that excites and challenges you. Also, if you're going to apply for a job, make sure it's a job you care about enough to at least do the minimum amount of research into the characters you would like to invite to your dream dinner party. I believe it was Richard Nixon who said this, on the day he resigned from office:

> Sometimes I have succeeded and sometimes I have
> failed, but always I have taken heart from what
> Theodore Roosevelt once said about the man in the
> arena, 'whose face is marred by dust and sweat and
> blood, who strives valiantly, who errs and comes up
> short again and again because there is not effort
> without error and shortcoming, but who does

actually strive to do the deed, who knows the great
enthusiasms, the great devotions, who spends
himself in a worthy cause, who at the best knows in
the end the triumphs of high achievements and
who at the worst, if he fails, at least fails while
daring greatly'.

Fuck, now that guy would be cool at a dinner party. Also, if you ever see an ancient Motorola mobile phone lying on the ground, pick it up, give it a charge and have a look through the videos. There might be some footage that will give you some much-needed light relief. Because what I've come to realise is that on that night I was the gnome and Daz was the squirrel, and together, even if it was for the shortest of moments, we helped 300 drunken squaddies forget that in a few days' time they were off to war. Now, if that's not top-quality light relief, I don't know what is.

CHAPTER 7

SNOWFLAKES

A Generation that Likes to (Political) Party Hard

As a young, left-leaning person, politics haven't gone my way very often of late, or indeed at any point in my adult life. I've never actually been on the winning side of any democratic vote I've taken part in. General elections, Scottish and European referendums and, of course, the 2002 *Pop Idol* final. Will Young. Will fucking Young. Gareth Gates had the voice of an angel and had been through so much! It still pains me to this day – I got the whole family to vote, for crying out loud! My dad nearly killed me when he saw the phone bill. 'We were trying to help the greater good,' I tried to explain to him, but to no avail. And don't worry if you didn't vote the same way I did in those aforementioned political votes; you are still more than welcome to read and enjoy this book. It is your democratic right to be completely and utterly wrong. I'm only pulling your leg – bit of fun, eh?

But seriously, if you voted Will Young, get the fuck out. You are not welcome.

'Oh God, here comes another young liberal not wanting his views questioned, what a precious little snowflake.'

The term 'snowflake' is constantly levelled at millennials. For those unfamiliar with what I mean, where have you been recently? Living under a rock? Or, even worse, not on Twitter? It's a term levelled at someone who is particularly sensitive, has an inflated sense of their own uniqueness and, as a result, does not enjoy having their beliefs or values challenged. There are a few theories about where the phrase originated, but popular opinion seems to be that it comes from a line in the book (and film) *Fight Club*:

'You are not special. You're not a beautiful and unique snowflake. You're the same decaying organic matter as everything else.'

Well, there you go, fellow snowflakes. We're all decaying matter awaiting the same inevitable demise as everything else ever created. You're not unique or special, as your parents led you to believe. Like Brad Pitt just made abundantly clear, you're no different to anyone or anything else – same as Keith, Claire, a shoe. We're all made up of the same protons and neutrons that will eventually perish and die, if they're not obliterated by the sun exploding first, that is. Except Gareth Gates, Jürgen Klopp and Charlie from Busted – they are gods among us mere mortals!

I find it interesting that the slur 'snowflake' is so closely linked to the idea of self-importance, one that has followed millennials throughout our lives. When we were children and young adults, this idea attached itself to our need to post online and tell everyone how great we are – we were known as the 'selfie generation'. Then we started moving into the working environment, where we needed to be a major player in an office almost immediately, which saw us labelled as the 'entitled generation'. And now as fully fledged adult voters it's progressed into the political arena, where we are seen as these fragile egomaniacs who can't have our views challenged, otherwise we'll run off and write an awful blog about how nasty old people are. Is that the case? It's clearly more than a coincidence that these accusations get levelled at us at every possible turn, but when it comes to the political arena there is far more at play than the simple fact that our egos don't allow our beliefs to be challenged.

Politics was never something that interested me – it is something that has been thrust upon me over the years. The most obvious and extreme example being the change in political mood following the tragic events of 9/11, which led to a war on terror being declared. Invasions followed in Iraq and Afghanistan, religious tensions rose and life as we once knew it changed for ever. Now, I'm not in a position to discuss the political intricacies of these events – I mean, a year later I was running up a significant phone bill in a futile attempt to help Gareth Gates win the inaugural *Pop Idol* – but their impact sent shockwaves around the globe that changed the political landscape permanently, and millennials were at the cutting edge of that change. We were on the road to adulthood, soon to become tax-paying, election-voting, functioning adults.

Like many of you, I remember exactly where I was that day. I had just got home from school. My sister had been off ill so my mum had stayed at home to look after her, and they were sitting on the sofa in their pyjamas watching telly. But it wasn't the normal heady mix of *Rugrats, Ed, Edd n Eddy* and the occasional music video, but rather scenes of complete and utter devastation. Even in that moment, as a 13-year-old boy, I knew that things were never returning to 'normal'. Not a chance.

And if you're old enough to be able to pinpoint your exact position that day, then you will probably be able to remember what airports used to be like before the attacks. Airport security used to be a place of chill and good karma. Shoes were left on, laptops remained in bags and two-litre bottles of cola could be taken on board to quench your mid-flight thirst without you being robbed blind by easyJet drink prices. If the terrorists' original plan was to make it impossible for me to fly my Molton Brown Christmas gift set back down to London without paying £50 for a bag check-in because it's over 100 millilitres and needs to be in the hold, then they've already won.

You can even tell which countries have had less involvement in international conflicts simply by going through their airports. I don't know if you've been to New Zealand recently, but that country clearly has not been through many long-lasting international conflicts in the last few decades. I mean, the only nation state they've ever had to worry about is Mordor, and they sorted those lads out in the space of three (admittedly rather long) films. These lads make Australia look like Fort Knox. I even made it through New Zealand security munching on an apple. I felt like Scarface.

Don't forget, pre-9/11, Osama bin Laden was a little-known fringe character occasionally popping up in some feature on the news, the United States weren't officially engaged in *any* wars and ISIS didn't even exist. We have decisively changed as a society, and we ain't going back, not unless we get our finger out at some point soon and win this bloody war on terror, which doesn't seem massively likely owing to the fact that, rather than being a person or state, terror is merely an ideology. That's right, we're at war and spending millions of pounds every year in order to fight an intangible concept. I'm not saying all these politicians and experts are in the wrong, but even at the age of 13 I remember thinking it could result in any sort of a victory becoming somewhat tricky. It's like one of us having a fight with boredom or indifference. You can try, but they're rather difficult to pin down. The war in Afghanistan is now the longest war in American history, with President Trump (never stops being weird typing that) promising at the tail end of 2017 to increase troop numbers in the region as a response to deteriorating security conditions. So it looks like these pesky intangible concepts really are impossible to get hold of – who knew?

The situations facing this country at the minute create real extremes in opinion. Things like terrorism, immigration and countless referendums are going to be far more polarising than debates about city-centre pedestrianisation or the price of milk. This has created a real division between our political parties, leaving very little middle ground when it comes to picking your political affiliations. We had the Lib Dems for a bit. Remember them? Oh, they were great, but Nick Clegg went and royally fucked it. I've not seen such a sudden fall from popularity in years – Nick Clegg is essentially the political equivalent of *Pokémon GO*!

Given that much of politics is being moved from private quarters, between friends and colleagues, towards the internet and in particular social-media platforms, you can see how easily these issues become more and more divisive. Gone are the days of nuance and debate; grey areas are for fucking cowards. Now you're either left or right, right or wrong, popular or Nick Clegg. Pin your colours to a mast, do it quick and make sure the whole thing is as public as possible! We need to know exactly where you stand on every situation and we need to know yesterday ... Oh, and by the way, your opinion is 100 per cent correct and fuck everyone else.

As well as the public nature and permanency of social media creating issues for balanced political debate, social media has another major issue. It is in every social platform's interest for users to be seen by those who share our likes and opinions. This means we get more positive feedback, which will give you that dopamine hit and encourage you to remain on the site. With things like music, food and sport this seems like a sensible and reasonable thing to do. I like football. I want to talk to other people who like football. The rugby lot can go take a running jump. The only time I want rugby to feature in my life is when I'm getting the landlord to turn it off in the pub because the football's about to start. I want all the build-up, I need to see Jürgen Klopp staring at the opposition – it's my official start to the weekend! What I don't need is all the rugby losers popping up on my timeline, banging on about scrums and touchdowns or whatever the hell it is they talk about. I want football on my feed and I want it now!

The problem when you apply this same algorithm to political views is that you create little pockets of opinion that go unchallenged, an echo chamber where everyone believes they are in the majority and correct, which very often isn't the case. Are we all snowflakes who don't want our political opinions challenged? Well, there may be some truth to that, but in the same way that our parents failed to prep us for the realities of the world in our adult lives, now social media is (intentionally or otherwise) guarding us from opposing political opinions and beliefs. We're not scared of having our opinions challenged – we just live our political lives in a cornered-off part of the internet where these challenges don't exist.

Truth be told, there are parts of the political landscape that make me feel like, as a generation, we have been well and truly screwed. If that makes me a snowflake, well, all I've got to say to you is, 'Don't tell me to my face, you'll hurt my feelings.' Take, for example, this statement of fact: my name is Iain Stirling, I'm 30 years old, I've written a book and I rent. Right now, you are reading the book that I wrote in a flat I don't own. My grandad bought his first house when he was 21 and he hasn't written so much as a haiku!

I don't want you lot thinking that I'm just another precious little snowflake here to complain about how hard my life is. There are some benefits. For example, I live alone, which is quite impressive for London. I mean, I'm no king, but I do live in a very special place that my estate agent recently told me was a 'studio apartment'. Or, as it's known outside London, a 'bedsit'. I live in a bedsit. I have no bedroom in my house.

I just wish I had got on the telly in the 90s. Do you remember people who were on the telly in the 90s? They were minted! Kids' TV presenters were loaded. Do you remember Richard Bacon? He was loaded! For those who don't know, Richard Bacon got sacked from *Blue Peter* for taking loads of drugs. He probably also had sex with loads of women. Some of you might think that's morally and legally reprehensible – I think that's financially not viable. I couldn't have a load of ladies back at my flat, I'd have no place to put them. I'd just have to send them packing while apologising profusely, 'Sorry, ladies, you'll have to leave. I don't have a bedroom.'

It's not as depressing as it sounds, though, because my bed isn't on the ground floor – it's up high. If your bed is on the floor there is something quite sad about waking up in the morning and being in your kitchen. I don't know if any of you have tried to pee from the edge of your bed into the toilet, but I can tell you that the really depressing thing is not missing, but actually how close I came. Luckily, my bed is on a mezzanine. Not a bunk bed, as many like to shout out to me at gigs. To those people I say it's not a bunk bed, the desk below is actually quite practical. It's a very efficient use of space for a small flat in the London area. It's a mezzanine. It's also a double bed, which is good. I only need one pillow, however, which isn't ideal. Have you ever seen a double bed with one pillow on it? Boy, it's grim. The real problem is that you don't know where to put the pillow. Put it on one side of the bed and you're admitting defeat, put it in the middle and it doesn't look right. It looks like a fat guy with a small head. I'm not getting into bed with that guy – he looks creepy!

The only problem is that I can't sit up in my own bed, thanks to its proximity to the ceiling. I have to army crawl every night into my own bed. Having sex is like going potholing. Do you understand what I'm trying to tell you here? When I was single I didn't have a single person back, ever. Not once! I mean, one-night stands are awkward enough – I would have had to wake up in the morning, turn to my lover and just say, 'I really enjoyed that,' and then drag myself out of bed on my back, feet first, like a sexy slug with a trail of silver slime behind me. Disgusting, I know.

The good thing about my flat is that it lets me know how famous I am. I think it's important to know how famous you are at all times. And it turns out that I am famous enough for it to be weird that I live in a bedsit. I found this out when my mate recently brought his eight-year-old cousin round to my flat. The problem with children is that they are very honest and have no malice, which makes everything they say sound horribly cutting. So my mate's cousin was outside my flat, and I could hear how excited he was. He then walked into my flat and it was the most harrowing experience of my entire life.

'Why do you live here?' he asked. 'You're famous!'

Have you ever had to explain the housing crisis to an eight-year-old?

Well, basically, mate, under the Tory government there started to be a massive decrease in the number of houses being built, falling from 300,000 in 1971 to around 150,000 in 1991. Despite this, the Tory government still encouraged home ownership the entire time, owning your home became the norm and everyone started buying their own houses. That was the British dream – to own your house. Every country has a dream. In America it's that everyone has an equal chance in life and everyone can own guns to end those lives, but in Britain it's all about owning your house. The law of supply and demand, however, meant prices started to rise and fewer people could afford houses. So to counteract this, in the 1980s Margaret Thatcher let people buy their council houses, causing a reduction in social housing. People who bought houses in the 80s started to see their houses rise in value, which triggered a change in thought process: you could now make money through home ownership.

The 90s then rolled round, and Labour took charge. You would think this would be good, wouldn't you? Come on, now, put that Nintendo

234

down. This is important. The Labour government actually thought they had struck gold because they realised people could make their fortune through property ownership rather than relying on the state. So they set up massive tax breaks on the now infamous buy-to-let mortgages, meaning the arrival of everyone's favourite person – the landlord.

Landlords didn't just buy one property, they bought two or three, and rented them out at three times the cost of their mortgage. They also had significantly more capital to invest than first-time buyers, so the average house price in 2007 rose by around £14,000.

That meant people had to move out of the centre of London to afford things like, I don't know, gardens – or in the case of some of us, bedrooms. So out of the city centre they went. That's what you do now, move out of town, buy a big house, never leave it and eventually die. It wasn't all bad news, though, because living out of town meant you could still travel into London for cheap – wrong. Thanks to a war in Iraq petrol prices rose, and if you're thinking of getting a cheap train ticket, well, they're privatised now – so fuck you!

So back into London we went, where prices had risen so high that had chickens risen at the same rate as homes since 1971, a chicken would now be worth £51.18. Meaning I couldn't afford a London chicken so would have to rent a chicken through the London chicken landlord. And I can tell you two things for sure about a London chicken rented through the London chicken landlord:

1) I'd be paying through the nose for it

and

2) the boiler wouldn't fucking work

At least that's my explanation of it. There is another argument that people use which is easier to say and takes a lot less boring research. Basically it goes, 'Blah, blah, blah, blah ... immigration.'

In fact, now that I'm tooled up with a few more of the facts, should I hear some disgruntled baby boomer bark this statement at me down the pub, my reply is now always the same: 'I don't live in a bedsit because of immigrants – I live in a bedsit because you bought all the houses in the 80s.'

I wish I had bought a house in the 80s. Buying a house in the 80s looked like an actual joke. And don't worry if you're a bit older and offended by that joke, I don't want to leave anyone behind. I just want you to close your eyes, think back to when you bought your house and remember how cheap it was. Come on! Buying a house in the 80s was too easy. Every day was like:

'Oh, Susan, you've got a third bedroom. I didn't know you were getting a third bedroom.'

'We weren't, but last night Craig found a fiver in the back of the taxi and we thought why not!'

Fast forward to 2018 when millennials get charged over a grand a month for a flat in London so small it makes children sad.

CHAPTER 8

FEAR OF FAILURE

Here Comes the Science Bit ...

We live in a world now where everything is sold to us as perfect. Instead of being told about self-worth we are sold the 'perfect lifestyle'. In the 80s, brands moved away from selling products and instead sold ideals. Naomi Klein, author of *No Logo*, referred to this as 'lifestyle branding'. Nike no longer sold trainers, but the idea of 'just doing it'. McDonald's wasn't just a burger in a box with a funny toy anymore, now the people in their restaurants are 'da da da da daa – luvin' it'. This is perfect for companies because when you buy the trainers/burger and are still left with that unfulfilled feeling deep down inside, the lack of that much sought after 'it', what do you do? Well, buy more of course, because we've been told over and over again that's what works.

Perfume adverts show perfect-looking models spraying scented liquid all over their abs and luscious long locks, sports companies show footballers living their perfect lives in pristine trainers and tracksuits, driving cars that you only see in the flesh at the weekend at a shopping centre where a company have brought one into the foyer to help advertise their 'race-day experience'. I mean, we live in a world where you can turn on the telly to see the most idyllic family enjoying the perfect night in with a fucking taco kit.

We have all bought into this lie that perfection is a goal that is achievable, and that's what seems to be the primary downfall in the millennial psyche. As Dr Linda Papadopoulos states in her fabulous book *Unfollow*, the issue with perfectionism is that it is very polarising. There is a very thin line between perfection and failure: you've either smashed your Mexican-themed dinner party or forgot to buy the peppers essential to the recipe because you didn't read the tiny small print on the packaging that states that half the ingredients for your tacos AREN'T EVEN IN THE FUCKING BOX, and what you've essentially spent seven quid on is a square piece of cardboard with some salsa and a few taco shells, which, let's face it, are probably broken. I propose a new law that no food should be displayed on the packaging of food unless said food is actually inside said packaging. I'm looking at you, Mr Old El Paso!

Perfection doesn't exist. By its very definition external factors are required to deem something perfect, and no one idea, lifestyle or delicious taco will ever be deemed perfect by everybody in every given situation. But thanks to adverts, social media, school, parents and the rest telling us things can be perfect, we try to attain this unachievable goal. This not only leaves us feeling like we are underachieving, but also that we are being judged and we just aren't good enough. We aren't adulting properly. I've experienced that feeling of doing adult life wrong on a number of occasions: filming with Jedward, holidaying with my family well into my adult life, walking into a hotel room with a shitting man, doing drugs badly in Copenhagen and being dry-humped in front of the army are just the examples that made the book. Believe me, the list goes on.

What we need to do is try our best. It sounds a bit la-di-da, and even as I write it I feel like a twee camp leader, gathering you all round a campfire to toast some marshmallows, which are of course gluten-free, but it's true. Instead of aiming for perfect, try to think, 'What do I want to achieve and how do I best go about it?' Dr Linda Papadopoulos refers to this as 'person-centred therapy', but it could also just as easily be defined as your 'why'.

As a comic I'm constantly questioning how to achieve perfection within my chosen field. Truth be told, what I do will never be to everyone's taste. Even with this book there are undoubtedly people who haven't even made it this far before deciding to leave it in their toilet on the off chance they get a particularly bad case of the skits one lonely afternoon. Hell, I might even keep a copy on me in case I walk into another occupied hotel bathroom. But if I worked from that premise every day of my life I would literally get nothing done, ever. Not everyone will like this book, it isn't perfect, there are bits I'm going to fuck up, and I'm OK with that. Essentially, 'person-centred therapy' is becoming happy with who you are

NOT F*CKING READY TO ADULT

currently, deciding what it is that drives you, and from that point you can then better yourself.

Once you eliminate this idea that your life should be like the family in that TV advert or like Hannah from the office's Facebook page, you can concentrate on you and find happiness within. You can then learn to deal with failure. Embrace it, become like the generation before, who see their past failure as the main reason they are where they are today. And, in case you remember all the way back at the start of this book who the inspirational rites-of-passage speakers were, it was Samuel L. Jackson who didn't star in a movie until he was 40, John Pemberton created his breakthrough product at the age of 55 – it was called Coca-Cola – and Aron Ralston cut his own arm off to avoid certain death after being trapped under a rock in the middle of the baking hot desert – he is now a bestselling author and had his life immortalised in the film *127 Hours*.

And with all this in mind, it's *finally* time to discuss the biggest fuck-up of them all. Ladies, gentlemen and everything in between, Iain Stirling's inability to adult properly proudly presents: the time he told an eight-year-old to go fuck himself.

THE DAY I TOLD AN EIGHT-YEAR-OLD TO GO FUCK HIMSELF

I received a call from an excitable member of the BBC's development team. They are the people who are paid to sit around all day coming up with exciting new ideas for TV shows that can be made for the wonderful British viewing public. Imagine them now, sitting on beanbags, drinking soya lattes, just hashing out ideas together. Saying things like 'No idea's a bad idea' and 'THIS, but not this'. It's an exciting world to be part of.

'*Strictly Come Dancing* ... BUT ON STILTS.'

'Ore Oduba can host.'

'AND ... he's in a tank full of eels!'

'Karen, you're a genius. Give that women a promotion!'

Now as entertaining as the idea of my good friend Ore hosting a show of waltzing Z-listers on stilts while water creatures brush past various parts of their anatomy sounds, not all the BBC's development ideas are good ones.

'Iain, we've got a great idea. *Live at the Apollo* ... but for kids!'

At the time I was both a stand-up comedian and children's television presenter, so it seemed ideal. I'd done stand-up gigs for children in the past, and they're always enjoyable. Normally four or five comedians in a small arts centre entertaining a small, attentive family audience. Enough suggestive comments and looks to entertain the mums and dads, but with a prima facie innocence so as to allow the parents to avoid awkward questions in the car ride home. So I gladly accepted the gig and started practising my low-end innuendo and knowing looks – this was going to be fun!

The day of the filming arrived and I made my way up to Newcastle. As I arrived at the venue I had the horrible realisation that a small arts centre with an attentive family audience was *not* what had been arranged. I found myself in a thousand-seater theatre filled to the brim with busloads of eight-year-olds – and I was the only stand-up comedian on the bill. I was also the headline act. Now, as brilliant as 'headline act' sounds to an egomaniac such as myself, I'm also a realist, and the line-up really undermined my 'headline' status.

First up, two men juggling fire – I'm the headline act.

Then the pop star Conor Maynard – I'm the headline act.

Finally, five pantomime horses, an entire gospel choir, and the pantomime horses are performing, and I shit you not, *Riverdance*. I'M THE HEADLINE ACT.

You can't even begin to imagine how much those eight-year-olds lost their shit at those pantomime horses. In fact, I'm sure some of you have taken a few minutes' break from reading this to quickly pop onto YouTube and see if any footage exists of this spectacle. Don't. There's not. I've checked. Believe me, I've checked.

To add to the already far-from-ideal circumstances, the development team in their infinite wisdom had decided that nobody performing that evening was to use a microphone, as using a microphone at a stand-up comedy gig would 'look messy'. I mean, thank God, I can't tell you how many times I've had comedy nights ruined by awful-looking, distracting microphones. So instead they gave me one of those clip-on mics – lapel mics, they are called in the business. You know, the ones you see newsreaders wearing, usually as they tell us something terrible that's happened somewhere in the world or something awful the government's done that day, normally linked to Europe, but I can never be too sure as by that point I'm too busy burying my head in the lovely liberal sand that is my Twitter-feed echo chamber. Those mics, well, aren't they fun? The problem with no microphone as a stand-up is that it results in you losing the legitimacy that really is required. With a microphone my performances amount to an art form; without a microphone it's a lonely man screaming about what happened to him on a bus. Children don't want to see that – I would soon discover.

I voiced my concerns to the development team, these concerns being: 1) five pantomime horses, 2) microphone-less, and 3) a theatre full of eight-year-olds. But I need not have feared. It seemed the development team were having very similar worries: 'Hi Iain, so the pantomime horses have gone down better than any of us could have expected. They're actually crowd-surfing. So, to give you a fighting chance, we've sorted you a grand entrance.'

'A fighting chance'. That's what someone at the BBC said to me moments before I went on stage to perform to a thousand eight-year-olds. And what would my grand entrance involve? Pyrotechnics? My name up in lights? What did they have in store? Well, you can imagine my surprise when the team produced a child's micro scooter. So I was to follow five pantomime horses microphone-less while looking like an eight-year-old with the world's toughest paper round.

I wheeled out, the music stopped, the crowd went quiet and then remained in that state of indifference for a good few minutes while I attempted my top humour/apologised for not being Conor Maynard. Eventually the room fell into a deathly silence. You could hear a pin drop, or in this case, an eight-year-old ask one of the ushers if they could go home. I don't know if you've ever tried stand-up, but if you can identify which specific audience member in a room of a thousand has politely asked if they can call their mum to come pick them up, you're having a bad gig.

In order to try to win over the young audience I tried some of my grade-A audience banter. I saw a lad at the front who seemed up for having a nice chat, so I opened by asking him his name. He looked at me, unflinching, and answered, 'Farquar.'

Farquar? In Newcastle, the only place that has more Greggs the bakers than Scotland? Farquar. But that was his name, so I was talking to Farquar, which is a sentence I never thought I'd ever say because I'm a human being, not a Disney character. After a few seconds of talking to Farquar I noticed that the room had gone even more quiet – how that was even possible was beyond me. It was like they'd shipped more silence into the room from another venue, where another comedian had followed another group of pantomime stalwarts.

I soldiered on for another five minutes or so, limply thanked everyone for a fantastic night and left the stage. And although those kids weren't a good crowd, they were at least a consistent one, and I left the stage to silence. The sort of silence they put in films immediately after a car crash as the main character stares out the smashed windscreen, clutching the steering wheel, breathing heavily. I knew it was going to be tough, but I couldn't believe it had gone that badly. These were eight-year-olds, they were used to sitting through boring assemblies involving the deputy head's favourite poem, and yet I didn't get so much as a titter for my razor-sharp observations about the school run.

I made my way to the dressing room and sat there, properly upset, that horrible cloud of 'you fucked up' hanging over me. All those questions you get after a tough day in the office swirled around my head: 'What are you doing with your life?', 'How did it come to this?', 'Do ten failed actors in pantomime-horse outfits have more artistic integrity than you?' I started crying, and I mean properly crying. You know, that sort of crying you do when you know for a fact you're by yourself and you think, 'Fuck it, I'm going for it'. The sort of crying you do when you watch *Up* on your own. When you know for a fact that you're in the house alone and think, 'I'm going to have a wank or a cry, I've just not decided which yet. Maybe both, how very exotic!' Have you ever been so upset that you've seen your own reflection and it's made you more upset? I was there. My friend Steve came into the room to see how I was getting on. He asked how I felt it went, which seemed like a daft question given the fact that my chin had now became a meeting place for my tears and snot.

'I just don't know what went wrong,' I said. 'It's just stand-up comedy without the swear words. I don't know what went wrong.'

Steve looked me dead in the eye and said, 'Mate, you done a big swear.'

The sentence hit me so hard I even missed the obvious grammatical mayhem of its syntax. Steve went on to explain what had happened. I won't even tell you what he told me. I will show you through the power of storytelling. Picture the scene. There's a thousand eight-year-olds, they're awaiting the headline act. I'm backstage without a mic, but armed with a child's micro scooter. I wheel myself on. There's a silence. I approach a child in the audience and the following conversation takes place.

'All right, mate. What's your name?'

'Farquar.'

'Farquar? That's a *FUCKING* great name.'

I then apparently just carried on with my set like nothing untoward had happened, like a psychopath who thinks that sort of language is entirely acceptable. Steve continued to regale me with the many ways in which this was a complete and utter clusterfuck and, as he approached the end of his story, I broke down. 'Fuck,' I screamed. 'Shitty fuck fuck, fuckity fuck.' As my expletive-Olympics continued, Steve and I heard the stage manager running towards our dressing room. Now, I can't accurately describe his run to you here, but do you know when a run is too loud for it to be good news? That. Do you remember when you were a kid and you had friends round for a sleepover, and you and your friends stayed up too late and knew you were making too much noise, then you heard steps coming down the stairs, but they were Mum's so that was fine? Then about 20 minutes later you would hear the undeniable heavy thud of Dad's steps and you would shit yourself: 'Run! Save yourselves! Quickly, he's holding a slipper!'

Well, the stage manager Dad-stepped towards our dressing room, blasted the door open and reminded me that I was still wearing my lapel mic. So, as a thousand eight-year-olds and, I'm guessing, the BBC development team were leaving the venue, their 'headline act' was screaming endless profanity over the Tannoy system: 'Fuck, fuckity fuck fuck. Go fuck yourself, Farquar. FUCK YOU!'

Not only did I die on my arse in front of a thousand kids that night, I apologised to an eight-year-old not only for the initial swear on stage, but also for telling him to go fuck himself over a Tannoy system in front of his entire school.

THE INSPIRATIONAL SPEECH MOMENT

When I started writing this book I was still working out what it was that I actually wanted to say about adulting, why millennials find it so difficult and why that gig in Newcastle had such a lasting effect on me. I knew they were all interlinked, but it wasn't until I talked to my mum that I had my much-needed epiphany. I had worried about sitting down with Mum for a myriad of reasons, reasons that seem ridiculous now, but when I listened back to our chat she summarised every point I wanted to make so beautifully and succinctly. It did result in some tears, so if you're listening to the audio of this book I can only apologise, I couldn't help it – it's true what they say. Mums really do know best!

IAIN STIRLING

We've talked for nearly an hour and I've not looked at my phone once.

ALISON STIRLING

Oh, yeah.

IAIN STIRLING

It's going to be such a good charge. It's going to be charged up so nice. What's the stuff that makes you proudest as a parent?

ALISON STIRLING

Because you've turned into a … I'd say a friend, but more somebody I respect and trust, and I think that's a good thing. I'm proud of what you've done and you do it with such panache. Things go wrong and you get frustrated but you do it, and that to me is what's important. You don't blame - if it goes wrong you deal with it, but you've had to do that so often because you're so bloody disorganised.

IAIN STIRLING

I'm so bad, honestly, you people don't understand.

THE INSPIRATIONAL SPEECH MOMENT

ALISON STIRLING

So you're used to things going wrong. The
big thing for me, son, is, you're a star in
my eyes anyway, but I'm so proud of what
you've done. You've done it because you've
followed your dreams and things haven't
always been easy

IAIN STIRLING

Yeah, I've done gigs to four people and
they've hated it.

ALISON STIRLING

Oh God, yeah. And you've come home and, I've
said to you before, it must be the hardest
medium to get involved in, and you've gone
there, out there, and you've dealt with it,
and especially when you've had friends'
children bothering you, and you've just got
on with that and dealt with that. The thing
that gets me, though, is the amount of
people who kind of find it hard that you've
done well or, you know, they kind of think,
'Oh, I don't know how he's done that.'

IAIN STIRLING
Well, thank you very much for doing this,
Mum, and thank you for being a wonderful
mother.

ALISON STIRLING
And thank you, son. I love you so much.

IAIN STIRLING
Love you too.

Embarrassing levels of crying ensued

Having my own mum tell me that she is proud of my ability to deal with the hardships I've faced will stay with me for many years to come, and for that, Mum (and, believe me, she will read this – the woman's watched over a hundred hours of *Love Island*), I thank you. I'm so used to things going wrong, and that used to niggle me, made me worry that I was doing adult life wrong. It made me feel like I was failing, but that wasn't the case. It isn't the case at all. The truth is, the fuck-ups are necessary and in many ways useful, so long as you take something from an experience despite its far from 'perfect' outcome.

Luckily for me Farquar found the whole thing hilarious, and his mother worked in an office that was 'absolutely obsessed with *Love Island*', so I made my apologies, recorded a voice-mail message for 'Glenda in HR' and went on my merry way. But more than being a very lucky escape from a lawsuit, that gig taught me what was important in my adult life. First of all, my 'why' – my purpose – has always been to become a better performer, to constantly improve. And by performing I'm constantly fulfilling that 'why', which is such an important aspect when it comes to fulfilment, that 'it' which seems to be lacking in so many of our lives. Second, it taught me that, rather than avoiding failure, you need to know you can face it as a functioning, independent adult. Ultimately, what I learnt that night as I screamed a profanity into the face of a child is that failure *is* an option, and a useful one at that. I've failed so many times, and with the benefit of hindsight I now realise that these failures have helped shape the man I am today. A man that voices *Love Island*, tells jokes and writes books. A man I'm fairly happy with – even if it took swearing at a child to work that out.

Ultimately, and pay close attention here as this is my inspirational-speech moment – fuck, this is so exciting I might even pop on a silly hat – there is no 'adult', no 'adulting', no 'adulthood', no nothing. No magic moment will ever come when everything in your life simply falls into place; instead you just carry on messing up and the only thing that changes is that the hangovers get worse. Once you realise that, Jesus Christ, life can be a lot of fun. I'm 30 now, and I can tell you this: adulthood involves cleaning a lot more cups immediately before use than I ever would have expected. I haven't even bothered to allocate a cupboard to put the clean ones into.

It's not a lack of failure that makes you an adult, but rather how you face the challenges caused by inevitable failings. That gig, and the direction my life had taken to that point, will always remain a low point – a fuck-up – but it made me realise my life needed to change. I embraced the fact that a full-time job in children's TV was not enough to fulfil my 'why', and fully embraced my passion for stand-up comedy, which not only saw my stand-up drastically improve but also helped me mentally. I accepted that first break-up and started to find happiness for myself, to actually like myself, without the need to rely on others. My workload increased, and more and more offers came in, including a call from the wonderful people at ITV2 to do the voiceover on a new show called *Love Island*, an offer I duly accepted, and the rest, as they say, is history.

It's not easy, and it never will be, but remember that everyone is in the same boat. There are little things you can try to do to help yourself: embrace rather than fear failure, have something in life that powers your 'why', and for the love of God try to stay off your phone.

This book has unwittingly turned into one of those inspirational speeches – and I for one am totally cool with that. In short, the years that followed that night in Newcastle saw me go from the lad who swore at an eight-year-old to the adult who wrote a book about it. Yes, I might have told a child to go fuck himself, but look at me now.

A TREAT FOR THOSE WHO'VE SKIPPED TO THE BACK

'The Millennial Circle'

When I'm in a bookshop I always have a cheeky flick through the final pages of any book I'm thinking of purchasing. I don't know why, possibly a throwback to my school days when I would desperately read the last few pages of the book I was meant to have read for homework, hoping they would give me a wonderfully succinct rundown of the themes and ideas within the previous pages. It never happened. So I thought it might be nice to do exactly that with this book, a rundown in a simple numbered list of why millennials as a generation struggle to grow up. I've dubbed this list the 'millennial circle'. If you want to understand it better, well, take this book to the till, purchase the bloody thing and then give it a proper read rather than hiding in the bookshop like a naughty little sentence thief! But don't worry, my 'skip to the end' brother and sisters, you can have a few more minutes to finish off these final pages. And I won't tell anyone if you don't.

1. Millennials are a generation who are brought up to believe that failure is not an option. There is a constant pressure to succeed FAST.
2. Parents tell us growing up that we can achieve anything, that we are special and unique. This creates abnormally high expectations from life.
3. Parents tend to over-protect us, meaning we don't learn about failure.
4. Schools hand out trophies and awards to every pupil, further confirming the idea that we are all winners.
5. We are brought up in the world of social media, a world that is designed to be about YOU.
6. The feeling of being 'liked' from constantly documenting our lives produces dopamine, which is addictive, meaning millennials all have an addiction to social media.
7. Social media allows you to filter your life to make it look better.
8. So even though you're facing problems you filter your life to look like the 'perfect' life you've been told your entire life you're meant to be living. Everyone else carries out the same filtering process, leading us to believe we are the only ones with life worries and struggles.

9. We then enter the workplace and suddenly discover the harsh realities of 'real life', which can be hard to cope with.
10. The lasting effects of the credit crunch mean we are scared to leave our job in case a better option isn't out there.
11. The 'likes' we gain from social media lessen our drive to improve our own working situation.
12. Lack of 'face to face' relationships mean we take to social media to voice our anxiety.
13. And repeat from point 5.

ACKNOWLEDGEMENTS

There are so many people I feel the need to thank and the acknowledgement section seems the best place for that, so here we go.

First and foremost I need to thank my friend and partner Laura Whitmore (calling you by your full name feels weird!). Laura, your talent is inspiring, your kindness infectious and your patience much needed (especially when it comes to a mess like me). Thank you for all your support during the writing of this book. I hope I make you as happy as you make me. I love you.

To everyone at Avalon Management – I can't name you all here, but let it be known I know how tirelessly you work and it will never go unappreciated. In particular, I would like to thank Richard Allen-Turner and Lee Hammerman, who always go above and beyond. To have managers I can call friends is very important to me.

Thank you to everyone at HarperCollins, particularly Vicky Eribo, for being so understanding and helpful during this process.

To Love Island and everyone who has ever worked on it – for being so kind to me and giving me such a massive career-changing opportunity.

To those friends I'm fortunate enough to have made through the comedy world. Steve Bugeja, thank you for joining me in many of this book's stories in real life, and also helping me to make them the funniest they could be in this book. Luke Kempner, a massive thank you for always being there to help me voice ideas or vent grievances; your impression of me always makes me smile. And Joel Dommett, thank you for giving me much-needed advice on the book-writing process and for that lovely quote on the front cover.

A huge thanks to Spencer Owen, Caspar Lee, Alex Bowen and Olivia Buckland (and my mum again) for contributing to this book. Your successes are inspirational to me.

The Edinburgh lot: Scott Patience, David Bruce, Kenny Stewart, Emma Stewart, Scot Dignan, Andy Kennedy, Dougie Meehan, Iain Lobban, Alistair Connal, Mark Robbins, David Watson, Michael Sadler and so many more. Uni years were some of my best years. That is down to you guys. I love you all.

My best friend Greg Black and his parents Anne and Keith. This book is about things affecting adult life and you have been there every step of the way. Thank you.

I would also like to make a final thanks to Scott Hutchison. Scott we never met, but your music will always hold a special place in my heart. I hope you are now at peace.